And God Said:

"Wanna See Something Funny?"

by
Salvatore LoGiudice

Published by Salvatore LoGiudice
Printed By: Lulu.com
First Printing August 2007 - Lulu.com

ISBN: 978-0-6152-0424-6

This book employs:
IFT®
Interactive Footnote Technology

Dedication:

To Kurt Vonnegut.
To Samuel Clemens.

Thank you.

Acknowledgements

Those who are blameless whom I love:
Mom, Pat, Dee and Shakey, Jim, Jamie, and Kareen.
Leena, Lori, Steven, and of course, the amazing Mr.
T., Grandma, Grandpa and Great Grandma Foraker
as well.

Those who are blameless whom I also love:
Linda and Bill, Kathi and Kristen, Chad and Ashley,
and Brian, *and* G.G., I am honored to have met you,
to have shared this planet with you. And James, Sara,
and Kyra-Rain, Michelle and David, and Lara, my
fellow of the east coast and lover of timely foods, and
Keith and Denise, Jim and Marie and Alex, and Scott,
a fellow thinker and fellow idler away of callow
summers, and Jonathan and Jerimiah too.

Those who bear considerable blame:
For William, for reading and encouraging. For
Virginia, for bothering with it at all when she could
have been gardening. For Eric, who applied his
considerable skills in English and writing. For Tracy,
who insists always upon art. For these, for their
kindness of having even given the poop valuable time
and consideration, and treating it as if it deserved
attention... and Carol too, whose canopener opened
these cans of worms.

And finally,
...Dad, who taught me Thesis by way of Antithesis.
You can stop now, I get it.

Table of Contents

Chapter 01 The Origin of The Science of Theoretics
Chapter 02 Gravity and NASA
Chapter 03 Might Vs Bright
Chapter 04 Meet Isaac Newton
Chapter 05 Meet Isaac Newton V2.0
Chapter 06 Space and Time
Chapter 07 Time and State
Chapter 08 State and Edgar
Chapter 09 Understanding Edgar
Chapter 10 Manipulating Edgar Part 1
Chapter 11 Manipulating Edgar Part 2
Chapter 12 Conclusion

Appendix I About the Author
Appendix II Excerpt from Vol 2: Religion

Chapter 01
The Origin of
the Science of Theoretics

Changing the names of things allows us to
redefine entire concepts. For example, when I
was a boy Uranus[1] was pronounced Uranus.[2] It
was renamed recently so that newscasters, people
from NASA, and others who wish to be taken
seriously don't have to say embarrassing things.
For example, if asked by some congressman on
some oversight committee what NASA has been
doing with all the money they've been given, the
NASA people don't have to respond: "We've
been probing Uranus,[2] Sir."

---

[1] Pronounced Urine-Us.
[2] Pronounced Yur-Anus

Certainly, this is not a new social tool. In ancient Rome for example, The Romans met the Gauls and promptly renamed them "barbarians." In fact just about everyone the Romans met they called barbarians. If they met a modern American, they'd call him a barbarian as well. Without doubt there is a respectable amount of expediency at work here, and in modern times it has been abused[3] by some short sighted individuals, however, in the end I don't mind.[4]

Renaming things, when used *appropriately* can help to clarify and even advance the concepts behind the thing being renamed. Renaming something can be used to provide a greater scope and a greater depth of understanding. For example, recently the act of renaming things was itself renamed to "reframing."

At first glance, "reframing" might seem to relate to the idea of "looking at the world through a picture frame," however with a little imagination "reframing" might be instead, considered to relate to the "framing" of a house. Suddenly "reframing" takes on a structural dimension that the word "renaming" simply doesn't convey.

As will rapidly become apparent, I am not a scientist. I have no advanced diplomas; no chalkboard; no chalk. I cannot convey my theories numerically, nor can I host symposiums due to an unfortunate bout of SAD, which also

---

[3] See also Handicapable.
[4] Since I can make some money with it.

keeps me from going outside, except when absolutely necessary.

I am, what may be politely described as mildly informed, or for those who prefer the negative, overwhelmingly uninformed. I am completely and without question unqualified to discuss physics or for that matter to write a book on the subject.[5] I am further handicapped by having only a mildly amusing accent, leaving me to pronounce "drawer" as "draw," and "quarter" as "quatahh." But, like all great scientists and writers before me, I have the hair for it and so, we embark.

I never really enjoyed studying. I have done it, but I must say that I have always preferred imagining things. As a result during my academic career I was of course drawn toward Sociology. Had I known, back in the day, that quantum physics was afoot, I'd have fudged my way through Newton and Einstein, and set myself up in New Jersey, the hub of all things quantum. Instead I studied Sociology at a substandard University in New England until we came to the boring numerical part, whereupon I wisely dropped out, and then dressed up as a mouse for a living in Augusta, Georgia. Suffice it to say that by this, nearly my 43rd year on Earth, I have accomplished little in the way of actual accomplishment. The bulk of my life's work is purely imaginary, or as I prefer to say these days: "Theoretical."

---

[5] Let alone invent an entirely new science.

My decision to become a Theoretician was a three-part event. Initially, it took the form of an amusement that occurred outside my therapist's office while I was having a cigarette. I considered the fact that my life's work was imaginary, and rather than admitting defeat, I thought: "Why not participate in the whole reframing thing? I mean, if it was good enough for the Romans *and* NASA,[6] then it certainly should be good enough for me!"

I realized that by redefining what might otherwise be more honestly regarded as imaginary as "theoretical," that instead of being simply an overweight loser, suddenly I was "reframed" into a wildly successful theoretician with a massive body of work to go along with my massive body.[7] I thought I might have cards made up saying "Theoretician" under my name in classy script and that I would explain that I had attended a theoretical university. At that time I certainly had no intention of writing a book on the subject.

Later that same day, I noticed that my bank account was growing threateningly low and I resolved to do something about it. But what? I had no stomach[8] for real work. Any decent fiction would require the kind of time and effort most people would reserve for important things like facts. While considering a government grant

---

[6] See also The Department of Defense.
[7] All this and a fat joke too!
[8] No fat joke here, sorry.

wasn't out of the question, I imagined that with my lack of credentials, along with the fact that my body of work was both imaginary and nearly inexplicable, that any likelihood of success in obtaining a grant was rather low. Even if I were to get a grant, then there would be the whole business of actually fulfilling my obligation, which I was in no mood to do.

I decided to treat this important question the way all important questions deserve. I employed a tried and tested methodology. That is to say: I looked at some porn on the Internet and then took a nap, confident that the answer would become clear at some future date.

When I awoke, some hours later, I found to my amazement that the answer had not yet materialized. As you will soon learn, all great thoughts come from drinking heavily on a train, bouncing up and down on a bed, or by entering into a deep trancelike state, which is in the end very much *like* a nap. Also there is William Shatner. I had completely forgotten about William Shatner.

While the answer didn't seem apparent to me then,[9] I did feel that I was on the edge of an important revelation. It felt to me as though one era of my life was closing and another beginning. I had experienced such feelings before and I can assure you it feels odd. It *feels* the way a locomotive horn *sounds* to a man with his foot

---

[9] No doubt because I had forgotten about William Shatner.

caught in a railroad track. While this may seem like an exaggeration to you[10] I can assure you that the title of the most excellent Ray Bradbury novel "Something Wicked This Way Comes" was very much on my mind that day.[11] At very least it felt as though I was on the blank page between the chapters of my life. It felt as if something great or something terrible was about to happen. Even then, William Shatner[12] was not at all on my mind.

I wandered the house aimlessly, ate a bagel, and looked at more porn on the Internet. Nothing was helping to distract me. Blank pages are like that though. They offer a world of promise, but nothing interesting actually takes place.

Later, slowly flashing through the seven bazillion channels my cable company offers, I unexpectedly happened across a television show I might actually want to watch. The History Channel was running a show called: "How William Shatner Changed The Universe." It was a lighthearted look at how Star Trek inspired an entire generation of inventors and scientists.

I watched.

Then it happened.

---

[10] It is. I am prone to exaggeration.
[11] Perhaps this explains the "train reference."
[12] Hang in there, I'm getting to it.

William Shatner asked and answered
rhetorically: "How did we know all this science
back in the sixties? We didn't. We made it up."

"Hey," I thought rhetorically, "I do that. The
difference between them and me is that they used
what they imagined to make money." I further
thought to myself: "I gotta get me some of
that!"[13] The magnitude of the statement: "We
made it up" hit me like...a ton of bricks. Like... a
Mack truck? Like a locomotive!

Fully understanding the importance of what was
just revealed to me, I slept. It was a restless
sleep. It was a sleep plagued with
incomprehensible visions of time and space. I
had a mission now. But this was a mission bigger
than me. This was a mission best left to the
universe itself or at the very least someone with
credentials. Perhaps even someone who wouldn't
be forced to check the box on an employment
application that said: "High School Graduate
With Some College." Perhaps this was
something better left to someone from New
Jersey? I tossed, I turned, I certainly didn't feel
up to the task. Inevitably I surrendered.

"Alright already," I said, "Life. The universe.
Everything. I'll get right on it."

---

[13] Okay I don't really think that way. I just figure it makes
me sound cool, kind of like a white and wild haired Will
Smith.

So it was that I began to explore the vast cavernous space I like to call my mind.[14] First, I needed to find a way to[15] communicate the legitimacy of my thinking. I needed a codex, a rule set of some kind that would allow me to "make things up" in a meaningful, significant and ultimately copyrightable fashion. This codex had to be holistic in nature. That is to say, it had to be applicable to every human endeavor, immediately accessible to the general public and it wouldn't hurt if I could include some degree of precision, even if it was a less precise version of precision.

This is how I was led inevitably to the invention of the Science of Theoretics. I know this sounds utterly absurd, but think for a moment; if Newton could be sitting under an apple tree,[16] get hit on the head by an apple,[17] and as a result, alter the way generations of people would think of the world, why wouldn't it be possible for William Shatner to hit me on the head,[18] and as a result inspire the Science of Theoretics? Come to think of it, that *is* absurd. It is absolutely and utterly absurd. Therefore, it is utterly and absolutely true.

While the Law of Universal Absurdity is not a *defined* law within the Science of Theoretics, it *is* an underlying construct, much the same way

---

[14] Please don't let all that echoing fool you.
[15] Make some scratch.
[16] Perhaps even taking a nap?
[17] This is fiction by the way.
[18] Also fiction.

gravity is an underlying construct in the Space-Time Continuum. It has been my experience that the Law of Absurdity is the life partner of the Law of Probability and together they conspire to establish that the more absurd something seems, the more likely it is to be true. Everything in this book is true.[19] Everything in this book is absurd.[20]

For example: People ask me all the time, what is The Science of Theoretics like?[21] I respond: "The Science of Theoretics is very much like a penis. You can bring it to school with you and no one will notice, however if you take it out in class and start playing with it, you'll be sent to the principal's office." While I personally have never done this, I think we can all agree that this is true.[22]

This is a brief but prime example the Science of Theoretics in action. The good news is, while there is plenty of logic and loops and the whole wild and wooly world of physics is included in the Science of Theoretics, there is absolutely no math at all. That is the wonderful thing about this new science. Math is not only unnecessary but also contrary to the goals of this science. So, we can leave the math to the people in New Jersey and instead start to have some fun with this universe of ours.

---

[19] Except the parts I've made up.
[20] Except the parts I've made up.
[21] I made this up. To date, no one has ever asked me that.
[22] See?

When they[23] have finished all their calculations and worn their chalk down to nubs they will find us already reclining happily at their findings, sipping margaritas and dancing the Macarena exuberantly. Please remember to greet them warmly as they are likely to be grumpy after all that math.

Questions for Discussion

1) Is "bazillion" an actual number?
2) Does any of this sound legitimate to you?
3) Really?

---

[23] The People in New Jersey.

Chapter 02
Gravity

We cannot begin to understand anything without understanding gravity. No one, as of this writing, can fully explain gravity. No one of course, except me. I am uniquely qualified to address this issue since, as I was unnecessarily informed by a psychic, Isaac Newton is one of my spiritual guides. I do not channel Isaac Newton in the traditional sense. Rather, he is sitting on the arm of my chair, pointing at my spelling errors and bad grammar and generally urging me to hurry up as he has a squash match with Jim Morrison this afternoon and he'd really like to get through this.

In case you haven't been paying attention gravity is vitally important. It's the force that keeps planets zipping around in circles all the time as well as the force that keeps us glued up against the planet Earth. Its importance may be further demonstrated by the phrase: "Perhaps you don't understand the gravity of the situation." You see. It really is that important! I don't think it's overstating it to reiterate that gravity is a big deal. It isn't the biggest deal of all, for as you will see there are much bigger deals in the universe, but as universal big deals go, gravity is definitely in the top ten.

When I was a boy I had a ball that was all blue and white like the Earth as seen from space. I used to hold the ball in one hand and a model of the Enterprise in the other and make whooshing noises. I would imagine that I was sitting in Captain Kirk's chair and my crew and I had just arrived at an amazingly Earth-like planet. Perhaps one with a society of gangsters or politicians.

One day at the beginning of summer, I was called away from my Enterprise missions by my parents. They had a surprise for my brother, sister and I. We drove for what seemed like hours to an amusement park, and we spent the day being slung around by machines operated by barely sober men my parents wouldn't otherwise have trusted.

All of this may seem to be moving away from gravity, but stick with me.[24]

So my sister and I get on the tilt-a-whirl and I apply my vast imaginary knowledge of physics. In order not to squash my sister, I sit to the right, explaining that as the machine flings us around centrifugal force will cause us to be pushed out and away from the hub of the machine. My sister being significantly slighter than myself would be flung into me and my greater mass would be able to absorb the impact with ease.

Sadly, while I was absolutely correct about the whole centrifugal force thing, I got the directions backward and when the machine slammed to life I was hurled into her causing her to exhale in a great gush and the continuous and on-going pressure prevented her from inhaling again for quite some time.[25]

My reputation as a scientist, having received a critical blow, never truly recovered. Fortunately, my sister did and we were able to enjoy the balance of the day, albeit on separate rides. This, what I have come to call the "tilt-a-whirl debacle," led me to take my scientific explorations underground. Spurned by my

---

[24] Hee-hee. Newton *hates* puns.
[25] I am convinced to this day that the drunken reprobate that operated the tilt-a-whirl had heard me explain about physics and intentionally reversed the direction of the machine.

contemporaries[26] and now regarded as a crackpot, I imagined myself instead a kind of evil genius. I would get a jump suit, an underground complex[27] where I would apply my genius by making a machine with a screwy-type-drill thing on the front to bore deep down into the Earth for some reason. I would also have to learn to laugh like: "Muah-ha-ha." For several months afterward I practiced often, much to the consternation of my parents.

As a side note: I never did get my underground complex. I attribute this to the short supply of minions in those days. I didn't get my jump suit either because Mom said I needed school clothes and not the Dickie cover-all that I wanted instead. Back then, it was just so *easy* to thwart evil plans.

Newton says I should get back to the point.[28] He also says while this is all very amusing[29] we are supposed to be talking about gravity. Oh I'm Sorry... *Sir* Isaac Newton. You know Newton, there's a reason they call that an honorific... alright, alright I'll get back to it. *Gosh!*

Sometime after the tilt-a-whirl debacle, there I was laying on my bed, ball in one hand[30] and Enterprise in the other when I realized that we were standing on the outside of the Earth. Just as

---

[26] Or at the very least my sister.

[27] Perhaps in a volcano somewhere.

[28] He sure is pushy.

[29] Sarcastic too.

[30] Stop giggling Newton! It's distracting!

if the Earth were a giant tilt-a-whirl, centrifugal force should cause us to be flung off and deep into space. Something was up, or wasn't, when it clearly should have been. In any case it was obvious that an experiment was in order.

I set the ball on the floor and a green army man on the ball. I spun the ball and fling...off he went. Then I tried with a matchbox car. Fling... off it went. I tried this with a variety of toys and each time the result was the same. I learned two very important things that day. First, whoever said, "Weebles wobble but they don't fall down," had never tried to balance a Weeble on a ball. Secondly, something very strange was going on; something amazing and exciting. Why wasn't the spinning of the Earth flinging us out into space? Obviously my experiment was flawed in some way, but it opened a question in my mind that seemed as vast as space itself.

Something was keeping us stuck to the Earth. This something was invisible, perhaps in some ways even intangible, but whatever it was it was ultimately potent. This "something" was more potent than the Law of Centrifugal Force!

Theories and visions sprang to mind, whirling spinning ideas that I can't, to this day, relate sensibly. What I saw there in that dimension that existed before my mind's eye, made perfect sense. It seemed right, it seemed like a representation of what was real, but it would need to be tested.

Like with all forms of advanced science, the applications of what I was about to learn would be significant. *If* I could learn how gravity worked, then I could also learn how to counter gravity, or perhaps even reverse it. Imagine! Starships, entire space stations even, simply *falling* into orbit!

I decided that I would need to duplicate the conditions of the Earth very precisely, and in order to accomplish that I would need a spaceship. Other than the Enterprise, I didn't have a spaceship, but I knew exactly where I could get one.

I sat down and wrote a letter to NASA. I asked if they had any spare space ship parts they might send along, so I could build one of my own. The tilt-a-whirl debacle had proven to me that I shouldn't explain about my theory. Instead, I would need to experiment covertly, and once I had overwhelming evidence, I could then address the scientific community at large.

As soon as I finished it, I brought the letter to my mother to be mailed.[31] Mom insisted on reading the letter. I don't believe she would have done so without my permission, but as she held the stamps and therefore all the cards, I reluctantly agreed.

She told me it was a very nice letter but she didn't think NASA had any spare spaceship parts.

---

[31] I didn't know NASA's address, nor could I afford a stamp at my current salary.

"Space ship parts are very expensive," she explained.

My father snickered and scoffed, which, as it turns out, were two of his primary skills, but Mom shushed him. She dutifully addressed and stamped the envelope and off went my request.

In the following weeks Mom spent a good deal of time with me. She was rather persistent in wanting to know why I wanted a space ship. I suspect now that she was concerned about my mental state. I was. after all, a rather strange child. I spent the majority of my time indoors, preferred television to playing in the yard and when not allowed to watch television, I would retreat to my room where I would have fantastic adventures in my brain, some of which I unintentionally vocalized. This included, but was not expressly limited to, practicing my evil laugh.

After a good deal of time, her gentle effort paid off. I explained about the ball and the army men and while the explanation was wholly inadequate and did not in any way reflect the depth or breadth of my thoughts on the subject, apparently it was coherent enough for her to understand. She told me that gravity[32] was what held us on the Earth. But what was gravity? Where did it come from? She told me that as far as she knew no one knew for sure, but that I could study

---

[32] Slowly but surely, we're getting there.

science and maybe someday, when I was all grown up, I could become a scientist and discover where gravity came from.

She assured me that this would require a tremendous amount of study and I'd have to pay close attention in math class but that I could do this because I was the smartest, sweetest, most wonderful boy, etc., etc. My Dad may have been a wreck, but I had a pretty great Mom.

While perhaps tried and true, Mom's methodology sounded like a time consuming and intensely boring way to go about this. The space ship idea was much more enticing so I decided that I would wait for NASA to send their spare parts.

While I waited, Mom bought me a few science books from the "How and Why" series. These piled up in my room mostly unread, because they talked about electricity and all kinds of things that weren't at all about gravity or warp drives or anything even remotely interesting. You could make a crystal radio - big whoop! I was talking space ships and they were talking *radios*? You could also make a device that allowed you to turn a crank really, really fast and make a light bulb flicker. Whoo-eee, be slow my heart! I didn't want to discover stuff we already had. I wanted to get at the cool stuff! I wanted the final frontier and strange new worlds and all that!

I knew that gravity was the first big problem that would have to be solved before we could get on about the business of space exploration. We would most certainly need a way to get everything up into space and to that end, an anti-gravity machine would be the first big step. You want to make an anti-gravity machine, you gotta understand gravity. It's just that simple. I had a really good handle on the problem, I just needed to test and refine my concepts.

Now that I had addressed my first big obstacle, that being the acquisition of a space ship, I realized that I would face another incredible and unfortunate issue once the space ship arrived. This was an issue so great that it could bring down the whole project. My realization was, that in the writing of the letter, I had inadvertently forgotten a critical component. I didn't have a gantry. I didn't *ask* for a gantry. How could I have been so *stupid*?

When I realized my mistake, I was sitting in the grass with my plastic Communicator, Tricorder and Phaser, which I had built from an AMT model kit.

I was outside because Mom made me go out. Usually she was content to allow me my own diversions, but from time to time she would force the issue and I would be compelled under the guise of "health and well being" to sit in the dirt and sweat.

There I sat, with bugs and nature crowding around me greedily, as I realized that perhaps I had ruined the entire venture by leaving out one oh-so critical element. Would I have to send a new letter? Would I have to endure another long wait? How in the world would I ever get into space and back before school started?

I slumped back into the grass, content to allow the bugs to consume me. My life's work was completely ruined. Dejection turned into a kind of fury and I balled my right hand into a fist pounded the Earth. I pounded while chanting over and over through clenched teeth: "Six, Six, Six," as I had seen Spock do on television when his emotions had threatened to overwhelm him. Surprisingly it helped a lot more than you might think and I kept it up until my Dad called out the living room window and told me to cut it out, I was going to kill the grass.

He told me to get up and run around and act like a normal kid for a change and to stop talking dirty. He had mistaken my chant of "six" for a chant of "sex" and this must have provided him with some kind of satisfaction. Perhaps he felt that this was somehow an echo of normalcy? I don't know. Anyhow, I ran around a little, until I was certain he was entranced by Hee Haw once again.

Once confident that my father was now fully distracted from me by Junior Samples, I sat down to ponder my problems and catch my breath. I suspected I was worried about nothing. This was *NASA* after all. You didn't get to work for NASA unless you were smart. Only a complete *idiot*

would ship a six-year-old boy a rocket ship
without including all the necessary accessories.

I imagined a NASA employee with a clipboard
gong through the checklist.

"Let's see," he'd say, "we got rocket stages one
through four, the capsule, of course, complete
with parachute for reentry. Rocket fuel? Check!
Space suit..."

Uh-oh another problem. I didn't tell them my
size. How would they know what size space suit
to send? Oh man! This was getting harder and
more complex all the time. Who knew figuring
out how gravity worked would be such a
bothersome thing? So many niggling details!

Well, the hell with it. I'd figure it out as we went
along, "cross that bridge when we come to it" as
they say. Probably space suits come in "one-size-
fits-all" anyway, but even if they didn't, I'd just
make my own out of tin foil or something.

If they didn't send a gantry, I'd just tie the rocket
to the tree right there in the side yard. It sure
looked tall enough. I got up and pushed on it.

"Yep," I said, "plenty sturdy. Yep, that'd do in a
pinch."

I'd have to use some kind of light twine,
something that would break away easily enough
once we had lift-off. For a moment, I imagined
the twine being too strong and sliding up the side

of the tree, scraping off bark as it went. The idea of hurting the tree made me sad, so I resolved to use as little twine as was necessary. So much for the evil part of evil genius? You might question the genius part too, but I was six after all, certain flights of fancy are to be expected.

Summer wheeled along as summers do, and more importantly, the mission deadline was fast approaching. I needed to have time to assemble the rocket, prepare myself and my experiments, get up into space, determine the nature of gravity, do the whole re-entry thing, ride back to shore on an aircraft carrier *and* get my school shopping done. All this with only about two weeks left? NASA was really pushing it.

One night, my mother came up and sat on the edge of my bed. She wanted to talk to me about the fact that I had been hoarding used aluminum foil under my bed. She had been very upset when she discovered it, most likely because it had drawn a wide variety of New England wildlife. She seemed much calmer now.

She asked if everything was ok. I nodded, my eyes wide, certain I was going to be in trouble for some inexplicable reason. You see, all of my actions made perfect sense in context, they were, point-in-fact, absolutely and concretely logical. Out of context, however, they seemed, well…odd; unusually odd.

"Why did you put all that foil under your bed?" she asked.

"For my space suit," I said, my eyes filling and my lips trembling.

"Your space suit?" she repeated.

I nodded.

"Yeah," I said. "So I don't die."

She nodded thoughtfully and smoothed the sheet.

She continued to ask me questions and I continued to provide wholly insufficient answers. I wasn't being purposefully misleading, it's just that at that age, I simply didn't have the vocabulary or perspective to explain that I didn't have the vocabulary or perspective to explain.

Later, laying in the dark bedroom, listening to my parents' voices murmuring downstairs, and looking up at the moon through my bedroom window, I wondered why people depicted the man in the moon as smiling all the time. He didn't look like he was smiling. He looked surprised, and maybe a little confused.

I imagined that if he had a cartoon bubble over his "head", it would say: "What in the world are those monkeys up to down there?" or maybe it would just say: "Whaaaaa?" As though the existence of our entire history and perhaps even our species itself was wholly unexpected.

Of course, that expression might not be about us at all. It might instead have something to do with the fact that God would occasionally and without warning throw a meteor at the back of his head.

I realize that it may seem to you as though I'll never get around to explaining about gravity. I assure you I will. Before this chapter is complete, I will explain everything there is to know about gravity; where it comes from, and how it works. Sir Isaac Newton himself, who is currently standing near the sliding doors that open onto my small and poop-filled patio, is here to help me remain, at very least, accurate, if not concise and to the point.

Why is there so much dog excrement on my patio? Newton wants to know. His hands are clasped behind his back, he is in silhouette, and looks quite regal.

"Because snow melts but dog poop doesn't," I reply. This seems to satisfy him and he walks over and taps my laptop with his forefinger. Wordlessly: back-to-work.

It was a Saturday when the first of what I was certain would be many packages from NASA arrived. In fact, it was the last Saturday before school started, otherwise known as Labor Day weekend. While for some, Labor Day Weekend meant trips to Cape Cod, Myrtle Beach or the Hamptons, for our little family, Labor Day weekend meant three uninterrupted days of my father's presence, humor, and other uncomfortable things.

The package was a large yellow envelope, which I thought certainty must contain an itemized list of the various parts which, no doubt, would be arriving by truck shortly, and perhaps a Saturn 5 owner's manual. I hoped that they hadn't gone to too much bother writing up the assembly instructions, as I had found that most things went together in a mostly self-explanatory way, and I was sure that a Saturn 5 Rocket would prove itself to be much the same.

The envelope was emblazoned with a blue and white NASA logo, which gave it a powerful aura of officialness. The whole family had gathered around the kitchen table as I enthusiastically opened the envelope. Inside was a type written letter on some official NASA stationary, a few large glossy photographs, and a sheet of cardboard to keep everything flat and smooth during shipping. I dumped the contents onto the table, filled with a mix of fearful optimism, and fearful dread. I shoved the photographs aside.[33]

I would re-print the exact letter here for you, but my father took all the pictures, the letter, even the cardboard and envelope to keep them safe until I was older. You see, the moon landing was the single largest and most important event in my father's lifetime. Perhaps this was as close as he had ever come to having something important

[33] An autographed picture of Neil Armstrong in his space suit, a color picture of Earth from orbit and so on.

involve him in any way. I don't know. What I do know is that I remember my mother telling him that the pictures belonged to me and him assuring her that he was only keeping them safe. They remain safe to this day.

As I recall, the letter addressed me as "Mister LoGiudice" which made me feel that perhaps they didn't know I was a kid. They thanked me for my interest, apologized for not being able to send any spare parts as they are quite expensive, and they need all of the parts they do have. They thanked me again for my interest, hoped for my continued support so-on, so-on...

It was over. Summer was over. School, soon to be known as "Ten months of living hell," was about to begin, and my space program was cancelled. As I am sure you must imagine, there were tears. In fact, my response to this massive and wholly unexpected disappointment involved a howling retreat to the solace of my bedroom, followed by curling up on the twin bed, and of course, the requisite "sobbing uncontrollably."

Mom followed shortly and cuddled and offered the kind of solace only good Moms can seem to generate. She'd have studied the pictures with me, pointed out important details, like Neil Armstrong *himself* had signed his picture expressly for me, as was evidenced by the ball-point pen impression on the photograph. But she had been unable to pry the envelope or any of its contents from my father, who smuggled it away for its long, semi-permanent "safe-keeping."

Later that night, when the house and I both were
still and quiet, I met Newton. He came out of the
closet. While today you might think that I mean
that metaphorically, in fact, I mean it literally.
My closet door opened, Newton stepped out, and
closed it quietly behind him.

Other six-year-olds might have been frightened
by the sudden appearance of a man from their
closet - most especially in the deep dark stillness
of night. But as I have already proven, I am
unlike others in some rather distinct and perhaps
unique ways.

Mostly, I wasn't frightened because I knew he
wasn't a man, not in the conventional[34] sense, but
rather he was just a ghost, and was therefore
completely harmless.

I should explain that among my many
eccentricities was the ability to see and converse
with the occasional spirit, ghost, and other non-
corporeal life form. I will likely devote an entire
chapter, or perhaps even an entire book to ghosts
and associated phenomena, let's just say for now
that the presence of the occasional ghost, while
by no means a daily occurrence, was common
enough that by the time I was six, it was no big
deal.

I sat up in bed, crossed my legs Indian style,
looking for all the world like a sad, possibly even

---

[34] That is to say: "Corporeal."

slightly bored six-year-old Buddha. I regarded him. He walked toward me, clasped his hands behind his back, and introduced himself.

"Do you know who I am?" he asked.

I shook my head.

"I am," he said rising up on the balls of his feet and settling back down on his heels again, "Sir Isaac Newton. In short, I am the greatest scientist to ever have lived."

I'm sorry, back to the present again for a moment. Newton now insists that he never said any such thing. But he did.

Yes, you did. Isaac, stop fussing. That's exactly what you said.

Why would I make this up?

No, that's just not true. I am not making fun of you. You said you were the greatest scientist *to ever have lived*. I remember because it's clumsy. "Ever to have lived" would have been better. Then I said, I thought that was Einstein and you sniffed. There, see, you did it again! Just like that!

No, no stop. Look can we just.. no stop. Can we just skip this part and get on with finally talking about gravity please? Please? Thank you.

So anyway. I was sitting on the bed, Indian style and Newton showed up and...

I know I was the one who insisted on talking about NASA, but it was an important part of the story.

Yes it was.

It most certainly was. It led up to us meeting, didn't it?

Well?

Alright then. Now can I go on please? They're waiting for the full explanation about gravity that I promised them. Do you want me to stop the chapter right here? I'll do it.

Yes I most certainly will. I'm the one with the body, and it's *my* laptop.

Yes, true. If I do stop right here, they will think I don't know about gravity, but whose fault will that be?

Yes, Yours! You're the one interrupting me.

Yes, you are. You're interrupting me *and* embarrassing me.

Ok fine, that's it!

The mass of the Earth warps space around the planet, and the effect of the planet's rotation ever so slightly twists space, causing it to press down against us. Gravity does not suck us down onto the planet, it mashes us down from above. All gravity is, essentially, is the side effect of warped space. It's like a ball wrapped up in a twisted bed sheet.

There! Are you happy now? I could have said it eloquently. I could have provided both anecdote and example, metaphor and fact. But there it is now, like so much spit on the sidewalk.
…

Oh don't sulk. Look, we're both a little tired and grumpy. It's been a long day. Why don't we do this: you go and play racket ball with Jim, and I'll...

Fine, squash. Whatever. You go and play squash and we'll both calm down and give it a fresh start in the morning.

Yes. Yes I promise.

Yes I'll explain about the apple thing. We'll both feel better in the morning, and we can get back to work. Alright?

Alright, good.

Ok folks, sorry about this, but we need to take a quick break. So enjoy your evening or day or wherever you are in time, and Newton and I will be back bright and early in chapter three, and we'll give this another shot.

Questions for Discussion

1) In what ways might mozzarella cheese interfere in space suit operations?
2) In what ways did NASA ruin my career and can someone sue NASA?
3) Why don't space ships look like the Enterprise when it's clear that we all really want them to? This *is* a Democracy isn't it?

Experiment

The following experiment is from one of my earliest scientific journals.

Material List
- Tongue
- Ruler
- Lips
- Lungs

Step 1: Stick out your tongue. It should protrude approximately one half to three quarters of an inch from your mouth.

Step 2: Press your lips firmly, but not forcefully, against your tongue.

Step 3: Exhale, allowing air to build in your cheeks until the pressure overcomes the seal.

Step 4: Note the outcome.

Chapter 03
Might Vs. Bright

The Science of Theoretics is flexible. It can be applied to any subject matter and is not restricted to physical laws. I had intended to discuss politics and current events in a venue more appropriate to their status.[35]

Instead, I find myself in the position of having to discuss these warm phlegmy issues here and now, since Newton has spent the past hour

---

[35] I thought I'd include politics in a separate missive, perhaps scrawled on a napkin, and then tucked into the finished book. My reasoning for this was that it would serve a dual purpose. It would serve to demonstrate my feelings for the current state of affairs and might prove useful to people trolling the ten-cent book bin who may have a cold, the sniffles or just something in their mouth that their internal organs no longer wanted.

animatedly regaling me with the tale of the squash match between he and Morrison and consequently has so exhausted himself that he has fallen asleep in the recliner.[36]

He would be hugely offended if I were to proceed without him. So we can just mess around with the Science of Theoretics till he wakes up.

I developed the theory of Might vs Bright recently while attempting to bring some kind of meaning to the 2004 Presidential election. Up until that time I had been fairly convinced that a politician who overtly lied and was caught in the lie would have to end his political career.

Repeatedly Mr. Bush made statements that he had never said any such thing, at which time the newscasters would cut to footage of Mr. Bush saying that very thing.[37] At the time I felt that this was most assuredly, what is regarded in certain circles as evidence. In fact it was the kind

---

[36] Morrison won. No surprise there as Morrison is young, fit and attractive and is just the sort of person you'd expect to win a squash match. Newton, on the other hand is far from the physical ideal required for success in sports. The combination of age, drink and his refusal to use "bobby pins" to keep his wig in place all conspired to seal his fate. Still though, the image of Newton in sneakers, shorts, and a tank top made me giggle a little and helped to keep the story interesting until he dozed off.
[37] Oddly enough, this fact was used to validate the conservative claim that the media has a liberal bias. I find it strange that *honesty* would be considered a liberal bias.

of evidence that if presented in a court of law would assure a conviction.[38]

The results of the election however, left me feeling as though something had gone horribly wrong. I don't mean to imply that something went horribly wrong with the election; I mean that I felt that something had gone horribly wrong with the very substance of the universe. Essentially a brick in the foundation of my assumptions of how the world worked had vanished completely, causing the whole structure to tremble and wobble.

Was I crazy? Was the world crazy? I spent the following day grasping at snatches and snippets of news. I was desperate for data. Like the little robot in that movie,[39] I needed input and I needed it desperately.

Amazingly, the news corporations seemed to understand that the election was in fact an aberration in logic as well. The lead story seemed to be "How could this have happened," or perhaps even: "What the hell?" In fact, I was rather surprised that the Oregonian[40] hadn't run that very headline in large bold print. It was the lone statement on the lips and minds of the

---

[38] The defendant says I never killed my wife, cut to footage of the defendant killing his wife.

[39] I don't remember what this movie was called, but it starred Steve somebody-or-other, an attractive young man with impressive pectorals and a pleasant personality. If someone from New Jersey remembers the title, please feel free to pencil it in.

[40] A newspaper in an unnamed state.

people of Portland[41] and the cause of their blank faces and numb shamblings to and fro. However, with their bosses still sleeping off their victory, even the national media crowd was able to very carefully approach the "What the Hell" issue that was on all thinking people's minds.

What they discovered and reported dutifully was that the "American People" were tired of "intellectual types telling them what to do." While a maker of vaginal supplies tried to sell me a product to control the odor of my vagina,[42] I considered that comment.

It didn't make a whole lot of sense, so like trying to determine the pronunciation of a word, I broke it down a piece at a time.

Intellectual types. Those people are typically called that because they use their intellect. People who employ their intellect are typically considered smart. People who tell you want to do might be, in the very broadest definition, considered "in charge." So, the "American People" were tired of "smart people" being "in charge."

I felt the kind of nausea typically associated with the first big drop on a roller coaster. It was a kind of "whuup" feeling where your stomach, preceded by its contents, travels up your esophagus and lodges between your lungs. I

---

[41] Oregon.

[42] At the time I had no vagina, nor was there one nearby that needed tending.

wasn't prone to physiological reactions when it came to other people's opinions,[43] but the sheer[44] brokenness of this idea left me pale and gasping ever so slightly.

I sat in my chair, breathing deeply and consciously. I was so intent on controlling myself through conscious breathing, that I paid no attention what-so-ever to what new and exciting products had suddenly become available in my grocer's freezer. I was unaware of which product deals best with "waxy build up," or for that matter where "waxy build up," builds up.

Though the makers of various products had thoughtfully spent billions and billions of dollars to let me know how I might easily take care of such common concerns as bathroom mildew, rust stains, under arm odor, and some kind of thingy that apparently crawls up under my toe nails[45] I remained ignorant, distracted by my current and very real symptoms.

After quite a long while, I mistakenly thought I had gained control of myself. I unwisely glanced back up at the television. Someone, a "news

---

[43] Other than the occasional stifled giggling.

[44] See also: obvious, utter, undeniable, overt, plain, and clearly discernable.

[45] The "thingy" in question is represented by an unpleasant looking and terribly rude cartoon character who invites his unpleasant looking and terribly rude buddies over to have a loud and obnoxious party under my toenails. I strongly suspect that this is not happening. However, I would gladly exchange it for the Bush Administration should the opportunity present itself.

personality" I suppose, had asked an "Average American"[46] what he thought about the controversy regarding allegations of certain apparent shadings of the truth by a certain candidate, and how those shadings may have "played out" in the minds of the voters. He replied:

"Well, he had to lie a little bit. If he didn't, he'd have looked bad."[47]

The room spun.

I collapsed to the floor, though I hadn't been standing.

I may have convulsed in seizures.

I'm really not sure what happened then. I most certainly blacked out. When I awoke with carpet fibers firmly imbedded in my tongue, it was dark outside. I rose to my feet and tottered about the room like a character from a George Romero film. I didn't know what to do. I was undirected. I had always thought that *I* was a little bit crazy, maybe even a whole lot crazy, but the world around me was ordered and logical, and for the most part, sane. Now, everything, *EVERYTHING* was in question. All my assumptions regarding the order of things, the origin of species,[48] the proliferation of life on a universal scale,[49] these

---

[46] Apparently discovered roaming a street somewhere.
[47] This is not fiction. He really said that.
[48] Alien intervention.
[49] Common, but widespread.

certainties and more, were reduced to frail imaginings.

Maybe the world was flat after all. Maybe it was flat and the edges were just further from Spain than any of us had imagined? Maybe instead of falling off the edge, you just appear on the other side like in some video games?

Maybe God *had* buried a whole bunch of dinosaur bones just to make it appear that the Earth was older than its actual six thousand years? Kind of like antiquing a table using a hammer? I imagined God gesturing toward the Earth as he spoke with one of His angels.

"Oh yes," he would say in an interested yet somehow slightly dismissive manner, "It's quite old. If you look closely, you can see a bit of the Pliocene era poking out of that little area I like to call Nevada." Polite chuckling would follow.

You see, it really was that bad. I needed to do something, I felt very strongly about this fact, but I had no idea exactly what I should do. I was moving in circles in the living room, and that wasn't helping anyone. I needed to express myself in some way. Yes. I needed to be able to tell the world that this... this... this what? Travesty? No, far too weak. Travesty is overused anyhow. Was there a word for what this was? I didn't think so. Usually, my instinctive response to problems involved thinking, but that ship had sailed.

It was perfectly clear to me that action was called for. What would Rambo do? What would Arnold Schwartzenegger do?

I would strip naked and climb to the roof! Yes! That accurately reflected my feelings. A fat middle-aged man, naked on the roof, howling of course and... yes.... yes howling, and when people looked, I would bend over and spread my cheeks at them! I would spread my cheeks and shout: "USA! USA!" Perhaps waggling as I did so. I was down to only my underwear when good sense started to take hold.

No, I couldn't do this. First, it involved going outside, a place I didn't like at all. Secondly, it wouldn't make my point. Even if it were given considerable thought, it would likely be misinterpreted.

While it did have the benefit of the "USA!" shouts, its political poignancy ended there. Further, good sense also told me then that any political protest I might stage should probably not involve my anus.

I don't mean to give you the impression that I am a skilled political protester. Point-in-fact, the only political protesting that I have ever done has been restricted exclusively to voting. I vote "No" on things that I feel are perhaps bad ideas, and "Yes" on things that I think may be, perhaps, good ideas. True, sometimes I just check "No," when instead I feel that "Are you fucking insane?" should be an option. But I don't want to make it difficult for the folks who count the votes by writing that in. So I just check "No" and leave it at that.

It was then that I caught sight of myself in the full-length mirror by the door. I was in my underwear, as I mentioned, but what I hadn't told you was that my underwear are Superman[50] underwear. They are bright blue and have the Superman logo emblazoned[51] across the front in brilliant red and yellow hues.

This calmed me down the rest of the way. It wasn't the underwear itself, of course. It was the idea that I was 40 years old at the time, and I *wore* Superman underwear. That calmed me. It reminded me of who I was.

I am an odd ball. I think I may have said this out loud for the sake of assurance. For a moment, I entertained the idea that instead of being naked, I could keep my Superman underwear on and instead of exposing my anus to passers-by, I could instead do a little dance, kind of like the little dance that computer generated baby did on Ally Mcbeal[52] all those years ago. But I was forced to ask myself: "Was this the action of an odd ball?"

---

[50] In case you didn't know, Superman is a Registered Trademark (or something like that) of D.C. Comics.
[51] I will try not to use the word "emblazoned" in *every* chapter. It's just such a fun word. So dramatic!
[52] Ally McBeal is a TV show that is probably owned by someone. Ask someone in New Jersey if it matters to you.

I also had my public persona to consider. I had spent years and years sculpting[53] my public persona to allow me the liberty to move about completely unnoticed. To survive in the world, I needed to be unencumbered by the kind of notoriety and recognition this sort of behavior would likely yield. Did I really want to throw away all those years of resisting the temptation to become involved? And for what?

No. No, certainly not. But still... the problem persisted.

I began pacing.

Was it possible that democracy was not simply fallible but inherently incompetent? I wondered then: "Why had there been issues over the rights of black people to vote, and issues over a woman's right to vote, but it never seemed to even enter the discussion that perhaps the real issue was in fact should the stupid be allowed to vote?" I'm not talking the merely dim here. They're alright. I'm talking the truly *overtly* stupid.

Let's see. First we'd need a way to identify them...

At that moment,[54] Newton leaned out from behind a nearby bookcase. He was soaking wet and was holding a towel around his waist. He

---

[53] Well, it has been more like whittling actually.
[54] Remember, this is back in 2004.

had closed his right eye as his shampoo had dripped and was apparently stinging a bit.

"Did you need me?" he asked.

"No," I said, "I'm working on politics."

"Oh good," he said, "I mean, yes, yes I see. Did you want me to get someone? Kennedy? Lincoln? Jefferson? Some Greek fellow?"

"No," I said, "I think I can field this one."

"Alright," he said, "I'll just... umm..."

"Yes," I said, "Go right ahead."

Where was I? Oh yeah, identifying the stupid.

If we were going to ban the stupid from participating in the decision making process, we'd need a way to clearly and objectively identify the stupid. But how? What things do stupid people have in common? Hummers? Hmmm. No, it's clear that *I* think Hummers as passenger vehicles are a stupid idea, but if *all* the stupid owned Hummers, there'd be no parking for anyone anywhere - *ever*.

Maybe, just maybe I could get away with the statement that "*In my opinion*" all Hummer owners are stupid, but not all stupid people own Hummers? Nah, the folks who make Hummers would sue the crap out of me. It would be *incredibly stupid* of me to make a target out of myself...

Eureka! Stupid people *do* stupid things. It's not just that they *think* stupid things like I do, it's that they *do* stupid things. It's inherent in their actions. It has nothing at all to do with what kind of car they drive, what kind of clothes they wear, not even about what kinds of pastes they slather under their arms to prevent odor causing wetness.

This would be a hard pill for the American public to swallow. The very idea that an individual's value might have a direct link to their actions, and may *not* be related to any specific product, merchandise, or fashion choice seemed somehow un-American. True, the individual value of any person *might* be reflected by their commercial choices on occasion, but in the final analysis, not even hygiene, not even tooth whiteness serves as an adequate measure of worth.

Perhaps, we could simply add another check box to the voter registration form. A clearly printed "Yes/No" type thing. Are you stupid? Yes or No. Only someone *incredibly* stupid would check the "Yes" box. The act of checking "Yes" would in essence self-validate. Genius! I had single-handedly saved democracy. And in mere minutes too. That had to be some kind of record!

Just as I was about to celebrate, my enthusiasm flagged. There were flaws. Big ones. This solution wasn't just a bad idea, it was an incredibly impractical and *ultimately stupid* idea.

First and foremost, the fact that the stupid don't *think* they are stupid would lead them to check the "No" box. We could make it a trick question of course, but I think that the intelligent and honest would likely also check the "No" box, and these are the very people we want in charge.

Further, if it got out that this was a trick question, then only the dishonest would check "Yes" and we'd be right back where we started.

If this was going to have any chance of success at all, we'd need a movement of some kind to help the stupid get a little more self-esteem, something that would help them to identify with their true nature. So let's see... A Stupid Pride movement.

They'd need a flag of course, something simple. Say, white stars on a white field. Yes, that'd be perfect. It would represent blinding stupidity.

They'd also need a slogan: "I was born this way." That'd do it for sure. That gives them an excuse and an aura of the scientific.

What else?

A symbol ... perhaps a cherub holding a bow and arrow - backwards of course. Perfect, that gives them a kind of religious symbology in a very appealing Hummelesque tradition. The image of the cherub would have to be surrounded with laurel leaves to give it a historic spin, and a floating ribbon near the bottom that brings us back to the point by saying "stupidus cupidus."

Once they were fully equipped with t-shirts, flags, buttons, and the various other pennants and standards, then they could hold marches in places like cornfields, select desert locations, and Lake Erie.

Oh shit! This was no good. I didn't want them to drown themselves, I just didn't want them in charge. I didn't want them commanding either a large nuclear arsenal, or money that was supposed to be set aside for when I was old and unable to work.[55]

The fact is, of course, that Social Security is a goner, it's done, forget about it. But we've been fortunate so far in that they have been unable to locate the nuclear arsenal since they are looking for signs that say "Nucular Weapons," but how long can our luck hold out? I mean, eventually one of us is going to finally crack and start screaming "it's NUCLEAR - that's NU-*CLE*-AR! Not Nu-*CU*-lar. You idiots!"[56]

Needless to say, I didn't solve the problem that night, nor the following day. In fact, it's now 2006 and I still don't have a satisfactory answer.

---

[55] As opposed to unwilling as I am now.

[56] Seriously don't *you* feel the pressure? I mean, Shit, it's been six years of this as of this writing, we can't hold out forever! Can we?

The Science of Theoretics does in fact provide an answer, but I'm afraid it is not a satisfying one.

What happened in the year 2000 and again in 2004 was not a fluke. It was not an aberration but rather, was an event of evolutionary necessity. Simply put, the stupid outnumber the intelligent by something like 957 to 1.[57] This means that, when considered on the level of species, it is the intelligent that are aberrations. Intelligence itself is a mutation being tested by the human species. The good news about this is that we are surviving. As we all know, survival is the test that evolution slips under the wet noses of all creatures, and we, though primarily dry nosed except on occasion, are no exception.

Throughout history, the stupid have inexplicably become feral, risen up and overthrown the well-meaning[58] intelligentsia. So while the Bush Administration may well go down in history alongside the fall of the Western Roman Empire, and the burning of the Library at Alexandria, we will survive.

There is historic precedence that, soon enough, the stupid will become less feral once again and go back to watching their toes wiggle, or whatever it is the stupid do, and we can get back to whatever it is we do. Just please, for God's sake, for the sake of all your children and their

---

[57] This is not a reliable number. Once again, please refer any factual or mathematic inquiries to the people in New Jersey.
[58] If occasionally a bit pompous.

children, don't correct them when they say Nu-cu-lar!

Well, Newton is still out like a light. That must have been one hell of a game. Until then, let's allow the old boy some sleep, shall we?

Questions for Discussion

1) Can anyone explain why impeachment proceedings have not yet begun? Choose one: Yes| No.
2) Please list four reasons a forty-year-old man might wear Superman underwear.
3) In what ways have the stupid become feral? Use additional paper if necessary.

Chapter 04
Meet Sir Isaac Newton

Galileo stopped by this morning to let me know that Newton was running a little late. Apparently, he got himself involved in a game of quarters with Sam Clemens and Pythagoras and he is feeling a "little under the weather."

I asked how he did, and Galileo chuckled and said: "Decimated."

"Well," I said, "I guess it goes to show that you shouldn't compete with Greeks where geometry is concerned."

"Nah," he said, "it was Clemens. The man's a shark."

I explained about the book and asked if Galileo would like to say anything to you, but he declined. He said he'd had more than enough of Earth in his lifetime, and wanted nothing more to do with us all. I tried to encourage him by indicating that we could discuss religion, but he just shuddered and turned me down flat. So I thanked him and told him to let Newton know that he could take his time.

It dawned on me this morning that there are quite a few real[59] theorists out there that might object to my reducing the idea of theory to something akin to "just making things up." I feel that it is important to clarify[60] that what a real theoretician does is come up with ideas based on facts, whereas what I do is come up with ideas based on experience. Any theoretician worth his salt backs up his theories with the kind of math most people consider hieroglyphic, whereas I back up my theories with anecdote.

Now, I don't want to seem as though I'm splitting hairs, since I don't know how one might go about doing so, nor do I fully grasp what the act might yield in terms of valuable result. But the fact remains that the two methodologies are very different.

---

[59] See also: Legitimate.
[60] For copy write purposes.

Theirs has the advantage of leading to real life things, such as Nucular Weapons,[61] which we can all agree is a very good thing indeed, whereas mine has the advantage of accessibility.

In many ways, mine is a new science. Certainly it has its roots in the more traditional, but it is unencumbered at this point, by anything even vaguely copyrightable. As the purpose of my sharing leads inevitably toward my bank account, I feel that I need to lay out a few simple rules, coin a few simple phrases, and generally make my work something that could be identified as having the distinction of "being something I could charge for without having to work too hard at it."

I mean seriously, how much money did any of the Greeks make on the square? Did Isosceles clean up in the triangle market? I met a man in Oregon who discovered a new geometric shape.[62] His is the first new geometric shape discovered in thousands of years! How much has he made? *Diddly*, that's how much! Oh certainly there is the whole "contributing to the body of human knowledge" thing; Newton's been living on that one for years now, but I'm talkin' here and now about the modern era. How do you think the cable TV people are going to respond if instead of a check I send them a theory?

---

[61] I just *can't* resist folks, sorry.

[62] His name is David Sterner. The shape is called Direct Opposite Reverse. There is info about it on the web.

And so it is with great pride and the desire for on-going cable service that I present you with the...

Ultimate Codex of
The Science of Theoretics.

At first glance, it may appear that the word "Theoretics" is only a truncated version of the word "theoretical." But, point-in-fact, it is the combination of the words "Theatrical" and "Theoretical."

Theatrics, as a stand-alone skill, was the province of my sister in the seventies. She was a Master.[63] I managed to learn the value of theatrics early on, training in them like a Taoist monk at the feet of Lao Tsu and before long, I became quite adept. But it was my younger brother who took theatrics to the level, not merely that of craft, but to the level of pure art form itself. He took to it like a sponge to water. That is to say, early on, he was dry and hard and appeared not at all suitable to the task, but as time passed, he really soaked it up, and before long, he was saturated with it. He could take the slightest offhand comment, contort it into the largest offense imaginable and report it to our mother in such a manner, with such style and heart-felt emotion that she would be swept up in

---

[63] Adulthood has seemed to strip her of these talents.

its grandeur, and weeping, she would call me from my room to chastise me.[64]

Further, I do hope you won't think ill of me for wanting to put a little "r" in a circle, or "c" in a circle or even a "TM" next to the words "The Science of Theoretics." We live in a world where the word "Smile" has been declared the property of McDonald's. Of course, the people doing the declaring are the same people who *own* McDonald's, but what difference does that make? If you don't believe me, go buy a pack or two of large fries and have a look. Alongside the word smile is a "tm."[65]

By the way, you're not ignoring all the footnotes are you? If you are, you'll never understand why my thoughts and paragraphs often seem

---

[64] All the while my brother would be standing behind her silently laughing and mouthing the words: "Who's the A-hole now?"

[65] Notice how slick I have become at avoiding lawsuits? Unlike the whole "Hummer problem" in the last chapter, this time I managed to say something that might be considered, in certain circles, under bad lighting and with glasses made with the wrong prescription as ever so slightly, one might even say marginally disparaging, while at the same time encouraging sales. I did say to *buy* some fries, not pick around in the garbage till you find an empty pack and then spit on the front window thus forcing some poor teen automaton to toddle out carrying an overfilled bucket of water and a squeegee to clean up after the impotent protest. So, McDonald's people, perhaps instead of doing things in such a manner that so clearly *inspires* disparaging remarks and then suing someone who simply couldn't contain themselves, perhaps the folks who decided to put a little tm next to the word smile™ might be encouraged to find more honest work?

disjointed. You see, I'm writing the footnotes in context, and then when I'm done writing the first draft, I will shift all the footnotes to that special numbered tiny print at the bottom of the page.[66] They are important[67] to fully understand and grasp the depths of the vast[68] concepts of The Science of Theoretics.[69]

Like all sciences, the Science of Theoretics™ follows a series of laws. These aren't your regular everyday kinds of laws, since those are man-made and foolish.[70] No, these laws are guiding principles that serve to distinguish these ideas from mere ramblings. They also serve to further distinguish "The Science of Theoretics"™ in such a manner that should someone[71] do things in this manner[72] I might instead be able to counter-sue for some unfathomable amount of money and thus would not need to write vaguely disparaging[73] things[74] to earn a living, but instead could live on a boat or in an extraordinarily large house with a houseboy named Pedro bringing me drinks with little umbrellas in them.

---

[66] Like this.

[67] Okay, not really.

[68] Okay, Not all that vast.

[69] TM

[70] Often having to do with someone's penis and/or vagina and who is allowed to put who's penis into who's vagina and how absolutely improper it is for someone to show their penis or vagina on film or in a photograph.

[71] Say, McDonald's for example.

[72] Such as utilizing an anecdote.

[73] If true.

[74] About McDonald's, for example.

So let's see... Yes. I really am making these up right now. Genius at work, quiet please.

The Law Of Point.™

The law of point isn't so much a guideline that requires that a point be identified, but rather, that the general motion of the anecdote indicates that a point *may* exist. Of course the Heisenberg Principle™ prevents any actual point or locus™ from being identified, point can be inferred from the general motion or overall direction of the theories in question during any practice of the "Science of Theoretics."[75]

The Law Of Diametrics.

As with the Physical Law of Opposition, the Law of Diametrics espouses the principle of opposition. Whereas the Law of Opposition states that every action has an equal and opposite reaction, the law of Diametrics states that every opinion has a variety of opposite reactions, many of which are unequal. For example, when discussing the Origin of Species, the law of diametrics allows for the possibility of Creationism, whereas any sort of rational thought would not otherwise allow such an obvious fairy tale to hold any sort credibility let alone be mentioned by adults... in *public*. I mean

---

[75] Let's agree now that all the words in this book are trademarked, that way I don't have to bother inserting all the little TMs. Also, if McDonald's™ then uses any word in this book (except of course McDonald's™ or smile™) we can really sue them for a whole lot of money. Well, not so much we as me, and not so much really as not really.

seriously, we're talking about *real* things. What's the matter with you people?

The Law Of Diametric Mass.

The fact that the concept of the possibility of inequality of opinion exists is critically important, but under no circumstances should the mere fact of opposition be used to determine the validity of said opposition. The law of Diametric Mass regulates the "weightiness" or overall mass of each opinion, thus allowing for something clearly and unreservedly true to have greater mass than something clearly and unreservedly untrue, even when multiple untrue oppositions may exist. Once again, looking at the Origin of Species, and more specifically, the Human Species, we have some clear indications between what is true[76] and what is untrue.[77]

The Law Of Holistic Analog.

Just as walls need a foundation to stand the test of time, so too ideas must have a series of support mechanisms to keep them upright and doing their job. But this is not merely a structural component of thought, rather it is a precise and intrinsic element which requires that the truth of "point A" must not only be supported by the truth of "point B," but the logical concepts of both "A and B" must be analogous, and in fact, form a coherent structure.

---

[76] Alien intervention, possibly in the form of a big black monolith but I don't think so.
[77] Creationism, Evolution from Monkeys, etc.

An example of this might be that the solar system, a big thing, is analogous to the atom, a very small thing. This is not to say that trees, for example, are just big fat pieces of grass, since that is clearly untrue, but rather that real things must in fact follow the same rules as little things, or big things, or for that matter, other real things.[78]

This is obviously a complex and subtle concept that could be discussed at great length, say at a symposium, or something in Prague where they send me a tremendous amount of money to blabber on for days.

Unfortunately, the same illness that keeps me from having to serve Jury Duty would keep me from cashing the very large check they would[79] like to exchange for my participation.

If you, like me have no interest in going to Prague, not because Prague is bad or anything, but because any sort of public thing involves the public, and you understand that the universe is holistic in nature, then you probably have enough of an idea to fudge your way through The Law Of Holistic Analog.

The Law Of Allowable Digression.
This states simply that digression is allowable provided that said digression has contextual validity. Said digression must serve to illuminate

---

[78] Somehow I feel as though I am not being terribly clear here.

[79] No doubt.

some aspect of point. For example, much in the same way I have used the phrase "for example" to indicate that the following statement(s) would serve to further illuminate some important aspect or another of those statements that preceded the statement "for example", so too must digression serve to illuminate the overall or grander motion as described in The Law Of Point.

Where the hell is Newton anyway? I know I said he should take his time, but I didn't mean it *literally*. I could have really used his help with the whole hologram thing. Ah well, I guess I should just be patient. He probably wouldn't have been all that helpful, what with him being hungover and all.

You know, it may seem as though Newton and I have a somewhat adversarial relationship. It's not true of course. It only seems that way because any sort of professional courtesy eroded away years ago. Are you familiar with the statement that familiarity breeds contempt?[80] Well, perhaps contempt is too strong of a word.

Newton and I are not at all adversarial, and we certainly don't hold one another in contempt. We are just like an old married couple that have been

---

[80] Do you hate that statement as much as I do? Man, it's such a bastard, isn't it? I mostly hate that it thinks it's right all the time. Oh sure, when I first met it, it was all cool and easy going, you know? But once I really got to know it, it became all clingy and overused. Before you know it, it was cropping up in trailer parks and truck stops - so cheap, so easy, so... pseudo!

together long enough that any politic that we would normally employ with total strangers has long since become unnecessary between us. We may snipe from time to time, but we do love one another. I don't mean love in the way a certain President of the United State of America would think, and then set about snickering.[81] I mean that we respect each other enough, and have proven ourselves to one another enough, that we can feel free to show disrespect to one another. You follow me so far? Good, good. I mean, if someone were to show up in front of my house carrying a sign that said: "Newton is a Dweeb! In big bold letters, I'd be sorely tempted to go out there -yes outside!- and say: "No, he isn't!"

The preceding was an example of Allowable Digression. Notice how it slipped into the flow of the dialog[82] and yet served to further illuminate the relationship between Newton and I,[83] a topic that is certainly an important and substantial part of the overall flow of this book, and therefore fully in compliance with the Law Of Allowable Digression and its relationship to The Law Of Point.

Remember Flip Wilson?

That would be an example of a statement that would violate the law of Allowable Digression.

---

[81] It strikes me that our <sigh> leader's emotional growth pretty much stopped at the junior level in high school.

[82] Well, monologue really.

[83] Or Newton and me, although almost certainly not me and Newton.

Even though it serves to further illuminate The Law Of Allowable Digression in context, out of context, say shouting it out in church, for example, it would in the end prove itself inexplicable.

Now, were I to say: "My father thought Flip Wilson was very funny." That statement might well serve to illuminate some of the sub-context within this book, in the end, just blurting it out like that would be a clear violation of The Law Of Allowable Digression. But don't take my word for it, you can try this out for yourself.

Remember, I said my Science of Theoretics had the benefit of being accessible? We'll, we've come to the accessible part of the class.

Each of you should split up into teams of two and head to church. On your way there, decide which of you is going to be the placebo and which the real deal. For safety's sake, I suggest that which ever one of you is *not* driving be dropped off a few blocks from the church. This will also allow for the illusion that this study is double blind.

Likewise, enter the church separately and sit in different sections.[84] Then at some point, perhaps when the preacher mentions "The Lord" as he is apt to do, the placebo can stand up and shout "Praise the Lord." Be sure to note the reactions of

---

[84] One of you sit in the bleachers and the other in the stands. Whatever. Just don't sit close together.

those around you. Most likely the reactions will be positive ones and some of the congregation may well follow suit.

Then, sometime later, the other should stand and shout: "Remember Flip Wilson?" Be certain to phrase this as a question. If you shout "Remember Flip Wilson!" it might well be misunderstood as a political statement and would consequently invalidate the experiment. Note the reactions. There are likely to be looks of puzzlement, confusion even perhaps shock.

When you compare notes afterward you should be able to see the results plain as day. Simply put, that a digression "in-context" is not a bad thing, whereas a digression "out-of-context" fails to meet its obligation.

Actually, on second thought, maybe you shouldn't carry out this experiment in real life. First and foremost, it is almost impossible to leave a church unobtrusively during a service, which means you'll pretty much be stuck there for the whole time. Secondly, while intensely funny in my opinion, it might be perceived as rude to suddenly shout out "Remember Flip Wilson" in the middle of a church service even if it does have the distinction of being phrased as a question. Finally, and perhaps most importantly, my initial instruction that each of you split up into teams of two is ostensibly a potentially dangerous proposition.

Each of you splitting into a team of two would require a tremendous act of will, one significantly greater than that required for standing up in a church and shouting "Praise the Lord," let alone "Remember Flip Wilson?" But on the off chance that you were in fact able to direct that force of will to the cellular level, it's likely to confuse your cells into actually doing it and you would suddenly double in mass. I'm not absolutely certain[85] but I'm pretty sure that the "suddenly" part would be unhealthy. In fact, I only suggested it because my elementary school science teacher used to say that at the beginning of the "lab" part of science class.

"Each of you split up into teams of two," he'd say. I was nine at that time, and I knew that made no sense at all. I watched him very closely for any sign of the fact that this was a subtle joke of some kind. I wouldn't have blamed him if it had been his own private joke, in fact I'd have found a renewed respect for him. He spent his days surrounded by nine-year-olds in packs of thirty or more; veritable *herds* of nine-year-olds. Why, if it had been a joke, it would have been almost elegant. But alas, it was not to be. This man was no Bob Newhart. Sadly, he had no sublime sense of humor, he was instead, just your plain old run of the mill idiot. <Sigh>

Of course, if you really, really want to do it... completely of your own volition of course, with

---

[85] Having increased in mass over time.

no encouragement from me, then fly! Fly, my bulky beauties! Muahh-haaaa-haaaa![86]

Questions for Discussion

1) Can you think of any social, religious, political or corporate organizations that deserve to have their knuckles rapped with a ruler for behaving meanly or in an inconsiderate manner?

2) Do you feel, as I do, that Ru-Paul might make a better President than the one that we have now? She's awesome, isn't she?

3) Using the laws of The Science of Theoretics as your guide, can you determine any potential point(s) as may exist in the preceding chapter?

---

[86] Me, Officer? No I was here in the lair all morning attaching this screwy-drill-type thingy to the front of my Impala. Why do you ask?

Salvatore LoGiudice

Chapter 05
Meet Sir Isaac Newton V2.0

I was just about to announce that this morning's session was cancelled. My thinking was that you'd probably had enough of my ramblings and without Newton to spice things up I thought that maybe you'd be a little bored. However he arrived just moments ago, so I guess we can proceed.

Newton and I have been a team of explorers since we met back in ... what was it, 70? 71? Newton assures me it was something like that. It was right after the Tilt-a-whirl debacle and the cancellation of my space program. It was a typical late summer night, the air was hot and humid, and also it was mildly dark. My room was only lit by soft glow of the moon, as I sat there cross legged and Buddha like, sweat making a slick sheen in the various folds of skin that I wore. Newton introduced himself and I said: "Hi."

As I have mentioned I was nonplussed. I had seen ghosts and spirits of various make and models before and had learned that they were for the most part harmless. The non-corporeal or "spirit world" doesn't have much interaction with us, no more than we with them really. Oh sure, we'd like to think that they are all floating around, looking in on us as though we were some kind of intriguing television show and they just cant wait to find out what happens next, but the truth is they have much more interesting things to do, and frankly, for the most part, we aren't all that interesting.

Some few ghosts are *trapped* between there and here and these tend to be the scary ones. This is because they were pretty scary in life as well. You see our souls, for lack of a better term, are an amalgam[87] of the essence of life itself and our minds.

---

[87] Much the same way Spiro Agnew is an amalgam of "Grow a new penis." Or is that the other way around?

Just as there is physical evolution to be considered there is also the evolution of consciousness. In short the universe and all of its associated and varied dimensions is little more than life piled upon life piled upon life. Wherever there is an opportunity for life, life occurs.[88]

I find it very funny that there are people who oppose this idea. The kinds of people who believe there is only life in our solar system make me think of a man who, having gone into the library at Harvard University and opened a book at random, picked a page at random, and finally having picked a word at random decided that all that is readable has just been read.[89]

Like the Harvard University Library, this is a very big universe filled with many, many words, and in all that unimaginable vastness there is likely to be at least one or two places still open at this hour. Don't you think?

I've learned that life isn't limited to just Earth and Europa, as many people believe. There are so many solar systems out there that... what? Excuse me a minute, folks, Newton is scowling at me.

What's the matter?

---

[88] This may exclude Mars, South Dakota and other places like South Dakota.
[89] As if the word "buttocks" was all there was to read!

Why? What year is it?

Ohhh. Crap. Well the cat's out of the bag now isn't it? I can't very well take it back.

No, it's too late I already said it.

Well what do you want me to do, say: "Ha Ha, just kidding there is no life on Europa?" that'd be a lie.

Look it's only a difference of like ten years or so. In the scheme of things that's not very much at all. So Prometheus One scoots out there, then those other expeditions follow and bingo. It'll be fine.

No folks, it isn't just corporeal life that abounds, filling the nooks and crannies of time, space and the rest of the dimensions...

What? Man! Newton, you are in one hell of a mood today, aren't you?

Yes you are, you're *very* grumpy. It's Clemens, isn't it? I told you not to do it, but noooo, you knew better. You thought it would be funny. He pretty much ignored you until you started the whole "twains-a-pain" thing. I told you he'd get back at you.

Yes, you're smarter than him, but he's witty.

Alright fine. I will. I will!

Once, I think I may have been ten or eleven at the time, although I may have been nine. Maybe I was six. I don't remember for sure. Time has gotten pretty confusing for me. Anyway, I was in the side yard with my dad. We were at the picnic table. He was listening to the baseball game on an AM radio that was roughly the size of Montana. The radio also featured the world's longest telescoping antenna. Needless to say, I was bored out of my mind. It was another one of those occasions where my well being apparently required allowing nature to feed on me.

Newton dropped by to see how things were going and we chatted for a while about this and that. I think it's important to note that by this time I had learned to distinguish between my inside voice and my outside voice. As I am sure you can imagine, using my "outside voice" to chat with someone that no one else could see caused some concern on the part of my parents and teachers. Newton had wisely instructed me in the use of my more subtle inside voice.

In addition to providing more a covert form of communication with Newton and the others[90] this inside voice was a significantly more powerful tool as well. It came in the form of both words and images. The images were fully illuminated concepts, images in full color. The idea of a boat wasn't simply the word boat, wasn't simply the image of a boat even, but rather it was the concept of all that a boat might

---

[90] We will meet some of the others in future books.

be. There in my minds eye, a three dimensional boat floated, complete with ocean and waves and large white sails catching the wind. Using this form of communication, words were, often enough, unnecessary. However, on occasion words might assert themselves to further the concept behind the image. I explained this to my father.

"Dad," I said.

"I'm trying to listen to the game," he said.

"You know what thinking is like?" I asked.

He sighed.

"What?"

"Thinking is like a comic book," I said.

He made a snorting sound and turned up the radio slightly. My cue to be quiet.

Several months following the events I am describing here, and for a short time thereafter, I thought perhaps that volume might correspond to intelligence in some manner.[91] I tested the theory by speaking very, very softly indeed to my Mom, and to nearly shout when speaking to my father. Initially, the results of this experiment were promising. I hadn't shared the theory with my brother and sister. But, independently of me,

---

[91] $k/x=y$ -or as the magnitude of one variable gets smaller, the absolute value or magnitude of another gets bigger.

both my sister and brother were soon speaking
very softly to mom and very loudly to dad.[92]

For example, we'd run up to mom and tug on her
blouse to get her attention.

"Mom," we'd say in excited yet very soft, nearly
whispering voices, "can we have some money for
the ice cream man?"
She would say, "Ask your father," and that
conversation would go like this:

"DAD! CAN WE HAVE SOME MONEY FOR
THE ICE CREAM MAN?" and then: "SHE
SAID TO ASK YOU!"

I told Newton, using my inside voice, that I
wished the Beverly Hillbillies was on.

"The Beverly Hillbillies are on," he said.

"They are?" I asked excitedly.

"Yes," he said, "the Beverly Hillbillies are
always on. Every episode is available at your
whim. You see," he continued, "just as there is
no spatial distance between two moments in
time, likewise there is no temporal distance
between one state and another. State, you see, is
indistinguishable from..."

---

[92] Proving once and for all that there are certain overt
truths that everyone can perceive, even without using
mathematics.

Newton was interrupted by some whooping sounds coming both from my father and the Montana-sized radio. Apparently, someone had done something amazing. In this case, it seemed that someone had hit a ball with a stick harder than most people hit balls with sticks. As a result, wild uncontrollable excitement flowed up from the stadium, was converted to radio waves, amplified and re-broadcast though a variety of relay towers, and was eventually snatched from the air by the world's longest telescoping antenna, converted back into soundwaves by the AM radio that was roughly the size of a territory seeking statehood. This in turn caused my father to "whoop." Newton glowered at my father.

"Must we listen to that infernal caterwauling?" Newton asked irritably.

"We could go sit under the apple tree," I suggested, a knowing and slightly evil grin playing across my face.[93] He scowled at me, but judging by his expression, an idea seemed to dawn.

"Listen closely," he said leaning in conspiratorially. "We're going to do a little experiment. Space, time, and state are all relative, you shouldn't think of this as a limiting factor."

I had absolutely no idea what he meant by any of this.

---

[93] Even at that early stage of our relationship, I enjoyed poking fun at him.

"Pay attention," he said, "now close your eyes.
Good. Start to think about what it will be like ten
years from now. Don't think about what the
world will be like, that's just the wrong way to
go. Think about what you'll be thinking about.
That's it," he said encouragingly, "just let your
thoughts travel through state. Excellent! Now tell
me what you thought."

"A monkey is president," I said, "like in Planet of
the Apes?"

"No," he said, "he isn't a monkey, he just worked
with one. What else?"

"Umm," I said. Words just didn't seem to gel.
The idea was there, but I couldn't seem to phrase
it, so I used pictures instead.

"Yes," Newton said. "Perfect! Wonderful! Now
tell him." He nodded toward my father. I
hesitated.

"He's listening to the game," I said.

"Tell him," Newton said.

I sighed.

"Dad," I said using my outside voice.

He didn't respond.

"Dad?" I repeated. I was sure I was using my mouth and vocal cords correctly, and he was sitting right there. We weren't more than two feet apart.

"DAD!" I shouted.

"What!" he exclaimed. "Jesus Christ! I'm trying to listen to the game! What do you want?"

"I had an idea," I said. I couldn't explain about Newton or the experiment we had just done. Dad wouldn't have understood about Newton, and I didn't yet understand the whole space-time continuum yet. So I pretended like it was my own idea.

"What if..." I said, hesitantly at first, the idea gaining words as it gained momentum, seeming almost to solidify in my mind through expression, "What if there was a machine that was like a tape recorder but instead of for music, it was for TV. Then you could buy all the episodes of the Beverly Hillbillies and watch it whenever you wanted."

My mind was alight just then with the idea itself, and all of the ideas associated with it. What had been vague and elusive was suddenly becoming very clear. I could see "the idea" of vast libraries containing all the television shows ever made. Each episode looked like a brightly colored paperback book. You could buy just one, or a whole bunch of episodes. I Love Lucy, Beverly Hillbillies, Green acres... Gasp! STAR TREK!

Or maybe you could just rent them. Like you rent books at the library,[94] maybe you could borrow TV episodes. Maybe even movies? Well, maybe. Movies come in films, but TV is like the radio... who knows. Maybe someone can figure out how to put film in the same thing like the TV shows. They do show movies on TV, sometimes so...

He should have been staggered by the idea. I certainly was. It was amazing, this was an idea with scope, a whole freakin' landscape of scope. Certainly, there was money to be made, but more importantly it was a cool idea!

Unfortunately, he wasn't impressed. In fact, he was *laughing* at the idea. Not laughing with joy at the grandeur, and not just laughing at the idea... but laughing at *me*!

"Ya dummy," he said, "Nobody is going to pay for something they can get for free."

I now believe that sentences can be roughly sorted into two categories. Sentences that should be said, and sentences that should not be said. One can usually judge the sentences that should not be said by the first few words of the sentence. These first few words are usually indicative of the overall sentiment of the sentence. For example, sentences that begin with the words, "No offense, but..." would fall into the Shouldn't category. Likewise, "You know what your problem is..." and most certainly any sentence

---

[94] You can find out many things about nuclear weapons at the library - look it up!

that begins with any kind of insult such as, "You ass," or "You idiot," and of a certainty, "Ya dummy."

My face darkened, rolled up and of course, there were tears.

"Nuh-uh," I cried, "You're the dummy!"

"Dunder head," said Newton.

"Dumb head," I repeated.

"Utter buffoon," Newton said.

"Baboon," I accused.

"Buffoon," Newton corrected me.

"Buffoon," I screamed.

My father stood. He was taller than me at the time but at that moment our fury met eye to eye.

"Go to your room," he hollered, pointing in the general direction of the house.

"Fine," I snapped, storming off, my arms stiff and straight at my sides. I let the screen door slam even though I wasn't supposed to, and stomped up the stairs. Just as I reached the top, Mom appeared at the bottom asking what had happened. I turned.

"Don't do it," Newton said.

"Dad's a poopy-head," I said. Clearly, I was more than miffed to run such a risk. But Mom just sighed.

"Don't say things like that about your father," she said. Notice that she did not indicate that I was wrong, just that I shouldn't *say* it. You see, sentences that shouldn't be *said*. Mom had sense!

"Did he send you to your room?" she asked.

"Yes," I said.

"Then you better go," she said, and returned to the kitchen.

"Whew, that was close," Newton said.

"You got me in trouble," I said.

"No I didn't," he said. "Did you want to stay out there listening to that dreadful ball game?"

"No," I said. Ahhh... I saw it then. Now I was where I *wanted* to be in the first place. Not only that, but Mom wouldn't be sending me back outside again. Pure genius! This guy Newton, he's like some kind of Einstein or something!

"Would you like to learn more about the continuum of space, time and state?" he asked.

"Ok," I said.

"Climb up on your bed and begin jumping up and down," he said.

"Are you trying to get me in trouble again?" I asked.

"No. First, if you'll listen closely, your mother has just gone outside to find out from your father what happened," he said, "secondly, we need a physical example that we can use to conceptualize the dimensions."

"Ok," I said and I began bouncing. Science is so much fun!

"Now," Newton said sitting down on a chair too small for him. "Please recount the nature of the first three dimensions." He crossed his legs, and interlocked his fingers together in front of his knee.

"Forward and backward," I said, "left and right... and up and down."

"Don't you mean depth, width and height?" he asked.

"No," I said.

"And why is that?" he asked.

"Because of relativity," I said.

"Excellent," he said, "you are already decades ahead of your contemporaries."

"...*and* I'm bouncing!" I said. I was starting to get winded.

"Yes," he said dryly, "don't spoil the moment. Demonstrate relativity please."

I began bouncing in a circle, pointing to the left with each turn.

"Left, left, left," I said.

I stopped bouncing. Now I was winded and dizzy as well.

"Now explain your demonstration," Newton said.

"Can't we talk about stuff I don't already know about?" I asked.

"Not until I'm absolutely certain you understand," he said.

"Alright," I sighed. "I pointed in a bunch of different directions and called them all left."

"Why was that?" he asked.

"Because left is always relative to my position," I said.

"In space," I added hurriedly.

"Excellent," said Newton, gesturing that I should begin bouncing once again, "and space is?"

"Space is the first dimensional super-set which is composed of three relative dimensional subsets," I said.

My mother called upstairs, causing me to stop bouncing.

"Are you bouncing on your bed?" she asked.

"No," I said, "I'm exploring the space-time continuum."

"Well, cut it out," she said, "you're being punished!"

"Ok," I said. I glowered at Newton.

"That time I was trying to get you in trouble," he said, grinning at me.

Questions for Discussion

1) How long has it been since *you* bounced on a bed?
2) Do you think it would be as fun as it used to be?
3) How might the world be different if the world's religions had developed a fun ethic instead of a work ethic?

Chapter 06
Space and Time

Time and I have never really gotten along all that well. This is primarily Newton's fault.[95] You see, back then I thought of time much in the same way as you likely do at this moment.[96] But Newton insisted that I learn about all twelve primary dimensions, or at very least get a grip on the first nine.

---

[95] Okay, okay. It wasn't your fault.
[96] A. What time is Star Trek on? B. What time is it now? C. And so on.

The biggest problem with time is that it is intensely boring. Space has the benefit of having matter and energy smashing around and making pretty colors. Space has aliens and big bangs and space ships and just one exciting thing after another. But Time? What's time got? In terms of excitement it's been totally short changed.

Scientists, throughout recent history have done their best to make time *seem* exciting. However, inevitably they end up discussing time travel which is a much more exciting concept, except as you will soon see, one cannot travel time without understanding its little brother (State) and before you know it, all you are doing is thinking and talking about state while time is just standing there uncertainly, shifting from foot to foot and feeling pretty much ignored. No wonder it's fleeting!

The second largest problem with time is that the more you understand it, the less sense everything else seems to make. Since we are all raised to believe that the world, for the most part, does make sense, when we encounter something that doesn't seem to make sense we cast it aside as frivolous and unimportant.[97] This leads us to the third essential problem with time.

Time has virtually no practical application. Oh sure some people say things like: "We're making good time," but by this they are really discussing space. Others may say: "Use your time wisely"

---

[97] Perhaps this explains the lack of impeachment proceedings?

but here they are in fact discussing the Tenth, Eleventh and Twelfth dimensions, which we will cover in a later chapter.

Since time has no practical application and the more you learn about it the less sense it seems to make, no matter how you think of it, time seems to be our adversary.

Granted it's entropy and not time that brings about aging, but entropy has hired a better PR firm and as a result there are plenty of creams and salves on the market that "smooth away the effects of time," but not a one to address the real culprit. Conversely, it is relativity that keeps all things from happening all at once and not time, as has been previously supposed.

So what is time? In short it is...

You know, I should warn you, once you do begin to understand time, you are going to very quickly begin having some real problems getting along in the world. It's very difficult, due to the holistic and interdependent nature of the universe to understand time without also understanding state, which then just corresponds back once again to space. If you are not very careful, this can get all jumbled up, and before long it becomes an obsession. At least that was my experience.[98]

---

[98] Or *is* my experience... or perhaps *will be* my experience shortly.

If you are like me, it will start as a very mild curiosity, an amusement really, wherein you'll start checking your wristwatch more and more often to see how much time has passed in a vain attempt to determine your temporal velocity.

Eventually, feeling frustrated, and suffering from a mild form of carpal tunnel, you'll abandon the wristwatch for a pocket watch, assuming that since it is so less convenient[99] you'll be able to resist the temptation to check it all the time. This will not work, as by then, the compulsion will be growing in strength by orders of magnitude and you will find yourself digging around in your pocket more and more often, and consequently, people on the subway will think you are up to no good.

Finally, not wanting to haul around that "lying son-of-a-bitch" all the time, you'll abandon the pocket watch, but by then, the compulsion will be so strong that you'll find yourself dashing into convenience stores and asking the clerk "When is it?" You'll get nothing in reply to that question but a perplexed expression, even when you clarify by saying: "When is it *now*?"

By then it's too late. You'll be unable to remember whose birthday it may be today; in fact you won't be able to know what day it is without help. Soon enough, you won't be able to distinguish between next Tuesday and last

---

[99] Most of our clothing is no longer designed with pocket watches in mind.

Tuesday making any kind of gainful employment nearly impossible.

Consider yourself warned and proceed at your own risk.

So what is time? In short it is the measurable difference in velocity between any specific twin locus in state and its corresponding twin locus in space. This can be demonstrated by considering your locus in space and state now, versus your locus in space and state..... now. You see? Time! There it was right in front of you all along.

You may be tempted at this point to dismiss this as frivolous. The simple fact of the matter is that while time itself does indeed have no practical application for us, by understanding time we can get at state, which does have some tremendous applications. Once we fully understand space, time and state we get at the really cool stuff. How cool? Well how about time travel, space travel, and something not unlike a transporter?

I knew that would get your attention! It's actually called a *Transtater*. The Transtater is more like the Stargate on the TV show Stargate SG-1, in that it is a stationary doorway that doesn't disassemble your atoms or anything... although it doesn't create a wormhole. So other than looking like a doorway, it doesn't really compare to the Stargate either.

It works by altering its own state so that its state on one side is where you are, and its state on the other side is where you want to be, and then you just step though. Of course, this takes a lot of power, so it's only used on each of the planets we inhabit and not used, at least not in the same way, for interplanetary travel.

Newton, please stop scowling at me. It doesn't matter if I tell them stuff about the future. First off, they are going to assume I made it all up. I've already taken care of that part. Secondly, it's not like there is some kind of prime directive we have to obey. Star Trek had a prime directive, *we* don't. The prime directive is totally made up. This means we can screw around with time and space all we want.

Well alright, you got me there. Okay, I'll do that.

Newton insists that we go back to the locus where and when the last chapter ended. He says that jumping so far ahead as to start discussing the Transtater at this early date, pretty much violates The Law Of Allowable Digression, and he is absolutely right about that. So to correct that, let's go back to...

I stuck my tongue out at him.

"Thinking of time as a single chain of linear events," continued Newton, "is much like thinking of space in terms of a single vector."

"Newton," I said.

"In fact," he said, "one must consider time utilizing the same relativistic orientations as space."

"Newton," I said, a bit louder.

"So we have up and down in time, just as certainly as we have forward and back, or left and right for that matter."

"Newton!"

"Yes?"

"This is getting kinda boring," I said.

"Well, I'm sorry you feel that way," said Newton with a hurt expression.

"Don't pout," I said, "Mom says your face will freeze that way and you'll look like that forever."

"That's patently untrue," said Newton.

"I know," I said, "but it's a funny idea."

Newton stared blankly at me for a moment.

"Kinda," I said hesitantly.

Newton sighed.

"How do you propose that we make time more exciting than it is?" he asked, adding hastily, "in light of the fact that your mother has forbidden bouncing on the bed?"

"Well," I said, "can we travel sidewise in time to an alternate timeline where I have a goatee and I convince myself to make my universe a better place by being good instead of being bad?"

Newton stared at me. Actually, he seemed startled.

"Is that still going on?" he asked.

"What," I said.

"That Quantum Universe crapola," he said.

I shrugged.

He looked off into the distance for a moment.

"Let's see," he said, "this is nineteen seventy something, soo... oh brother they haven't really gotten rolling yet." He sighed.

"Alright," he continued, seeming to get more and more worked up as he went along, "if you remember nothing else, then remember this: it's called *Universe*, not Polyverse! Every decision does not lead to multiple universes all formed and ready to go, complete with histories and everything."

"Don't get mad at me," I said, "I didn't do it."

"I mean *really*," he wasn't quite shouting but he was getting red-faced, "as if reality has nothing to do but sit around waiting for you lot to make up your minds. That's the problem with relativity. It's all me, me, me. Like you're the center of the universe or something. It only *seems* like you're the center of the universe!

"Can you remember this," he said, turning and pointing at me, "There is only one reality. Any idea that deviates from that is pure intellectual masturbation."

"One reality. Masturbation," I said, "got it."

"Good," he said. He paused, seeming to realize what I just said.

"Mmm," he said thoughtfully, "You probably shouldn't explain it to your mother that way."

"Ok," I said.

"Now, back to the problem at hand," he said brightly. "How in the world will we make time more interesting?"

I didn't say anything because I didn't want to send him flying off the handle again. He thought about it, pacing back and forth and finally turned to me.

"You know," he said, "some of your future states have been poking around back here. We could put that to use. We could form a bridge between a more current group of states and those future groups, and you could have a conversation with yourself."

"Mom says talkin to yourself makes people nervous," I said.

"Right she is," said Newton, "and it's potentially dangerous as well, but this kind of talking to yourself will be interesting. It's very much like time travel."

"Ok," I said. I brightened a bit.

"Still though," he said, "I'm not certain how it will clarify time. Just because you walk around in space doesn't mean you understand space. Perhaps it would be better if I just explained time and leave it at that."

"Time travel sounds a lot more interesting to me," I said, fearing another long lecture.

"In order to understand the three dimensional nature of time," he said, ignoring my comment, "you should think of time as being similar to space. Understand, I am speaking figuratively when I say that events, like matter, exist for you to interact with. Your decisions lead you closer to a particular event or further away from a particular event much in the same way your motion in space alters what matter you interact with."

"Newton," I said.

"In reality of course, it's not so much that events pre-exist, but rather shall we say, events pre-exist in a state of probability relative to your state in time and space," he said, "and in relationship..."

"Boring alert. Boring alert," I said, "All hands, prepare for boring." I started making a "Braaap! Braaap!" sound like the "red alert" klaxon on the Enterprise.

"Stop that," Newton said, "this is not boring. I am clearly explaining the three dimensional nature of time."

"Do you know how I know this is boring?" I asked.

"No," said Newton.

"Cause it's *boring*," I said laughing.

Newton tried to hide the fact that he found this as funny as I did. He was only marginally successful.

"Well, what is it you'd like to do instead," he said.

"I want to time travel," I said.

"It's a little dangerous," Newton said.

"Will it hurt?" I asked.

"No," Newton said, "but it may leave you thinking in a funny way."

"That's it?" I asked.

"Yeah, pretty much," he said.

"Let's do it," I said.

Questions for Discussion

1) Considering that it is relativity and not time that keeps things from happening all at once, can you name one good use for time?

2) If an employee got on a train in Los Angeles at 8:00 AM and traveled to New York at a rate of 3,000 MPH he would disembark at 6:00 AM. How might this improve productivity?

Salvatore LoGiudice

Chapter 07
Time and State

The following takes place in real time.

I eased back onto my bed and closed my eyes.
Newton paced back and forth encouraging me.

"Earlier," he said, "we accessed state in a passive
manner. This time, we'll be taking a more active
role and establishing a dialog."

"And it wont hurt?" I asked.

"No," he said, "likely not."

"Likely?" I asked, opening my eyes and sitting up in alarm.

"Relax," he said, easing me back, "and concentrate. Think toward yourself, but in the future. This is going to take quite a bit of effort..."

"Hello," I said.

"Hello," I replied.

"I think I got me on the first try," I said.

"Really," Newton said, "that's ama... I mean I knew you could do it. Ask yourself something."

"Tell me something I should know about the future," I said.

"Buy Microsoft," I replied.

"I said buy Microscopes," I said.

"No, no," I said, "I mean quit college and buy Microsoft stock."

"Now I said I should quit school first, then buy microscope stockings," I said, sitting up and looking at Newton.

"Hmm," Newton said, looking seriously at me.

"Do they let you do that?" I asked.

"Do what?" Newton asked.

"Yes," I said.

"Quit school?" I asked.

"No," Newton said.

I looked over at Newton.

"Do you remember when we tried to communicate with me in the future?" I asked. He nodded at me.

"I was saying buy Microsoft stock, not microscope stockings," I said.

Newton says that makes a lot more sense. I have to say I agree. I had wondered why I had told myself to buy what I had imagined to be "microscope cozies" for the longest time. Now I understand.

"Is there a moon base?" I asked.

"No," I said.

"Starships?" I asked.

"No," I said, "there's an International Space Station though."

"But no starships," I said.

"Nope," I said," But listen. Buy Microsoft not microscopes. Micro-SOFT."

I looked at Newton and sighed.

"I said *soft*," I said, "and there are no starships."

"We should write this down," Newton said.

"I am," I said, "and you are there too."

"That's good to know," Newton said, "ask what the future is like."

"Tell me about the future," I said.

"Well," I said, "an idiot is President, there's a hole in the ozone layer and the north pole has started melting. We have personal computers and cell phones and wireless networks, also cable TV and DVDs and Tivo."

"I said," I said, "an idiot is President, there's a hole in the air, and Santa's house fell in the ocean. Everyone has computers and communicators and... something called TVO. What's TVO?"

"It's a machine that records TV so that you can watch whatever shows you want, whenever you want," I said.

"Whoo-hoooo," I shouted, leaping to my feet. I held my arms up marching up and down on the bed, "I was right, I was right!"

"Yes," said Newton, "and it seems that your father bears an uncanny resemblance to the future President of the United States."

"Ha ha," I said, "I was right."

As I recall, at that moment Mom called upstairs announcing supper, and the experiment ended.

Well, at the time I thought it had ended, the truth was it hadn't ended at all, rather instead it continued thirty-one years later, and three years later, and three years before, and again twenty years after that, and eight years after that as well. Now that time was like three dimensional space and I could move freely through it much in the same way I could move in space, the exact when of specific events started getting a bit convoluted. In fact, all of time has become quite dizzying to me.

"I do wish you would clean that up," Newton said. He had walked back over to the sliding doors and was looking at the dog poop on the patio.

"You clean it up," I said, "you're always hanging around, you don't pay rent, you talk through my TV shows and only shut up during the commercials... what's up with that?"

"The commercials are louder," he said, "and as to the matter of my contribution, have we forgotten that I have contributed to the overall body of human knowledge? How many people do you know that have an entire paradigm named after them?"

"It's not the entire paradigm," I said, "you have to share it with Descartes. And Newton?"

"Yes," he said.

"You're talking directly into the book," I said.

"Yes," he said.

"In the present," I said.

"Yes," he said. "I suppose so, although it really isn't the present, it's the past."

"It is?" I asked.

"Yes," he said, pointing at the screen. "Look at your tense. All past tense."

"I suppose so," I said.

"The present doesn't actually exist," he said, "while at the same time it exists at all locus in time. It's a concept that seems to hover on the brink between the past and the future while, not coincidentally I might add, existing in all moments of the past and future simultaneously."

"Not coincidentally?" I asked.

"Yes," he said.

"So... by design?"

Newton sighed at me and put his hands on his hips.

"Yes, by design. But don't go starting any religions."

"So it was God?" I asked.

"Well," he said pausing a moment, "Yes, it was God."

"So there is a God," I said, "a God who created the universe."

"Yes," Newton said sitting back down in the recliner again. "What is it about this that's confusing to you?"

"What's God like?" I asked.

"Nice," Newton said, "great sense of humor."

"Nice," I said, "God is *nice*? Is that all? I find out God is real and all you can say is that God is nice."

"Very nice actually," Newton said, "and very smart too."

"Is God a man or woman?" I asked.

"Don't be an idiot," he said, "God is much like you."

"Me?"

"Not you specifically," he said, "You as a species. But also, not exactly."

"I don't understand," I said.

"Ahh," Newton said, "now we are getting somewhere... figuratively speaking."

"We are?" I asked.

"Yes," he said, "it's a question of state."

"So, my state isn't capable of understanding it yet?" I asked.

"No," he said, waving his hands dismissively, "it's not that at all. This is why understanding state is important. Once you understand state, then you can understand the tenth, eleventh and twelfth dimensions of consciousness, with that clearly in mind..."

"Consciousness?" I asked.

"No. Cognition," Newton said.

"Cognition," I said.

"No," he said, sounding frustrated, "Pay attention! Cognition!"

"That's what I just said," I said.

"Listen to me very closely," he said, leaning forward. "Do you remember all those years ago when you thought you said microscope?"

"Yes," I said.

"This is essentially the same problem," he said.

Questions for Discussion

1) If a man, living alone on an island in the year 2006 were to have written the book of Revelation, do you think it might still be included in the Gospel?
2) To help understand the dimension beyond state, please take a moment to consider what the word "Edgar" means to you.

Salvatore LoGiudice

Chapter 08
State and Edgar

While it may not seem clear at first,[100] it is only appropriate and fair that we designate the tenth, eleventh and twelfth dimensions as "Edgar." I was of course tempted to name it after myself, but I'd never be able to take myself seriously again if I did. Likewise, the guy that's running around, patting himself on the back and claiming that he discovered the reason for the big bang by adding in the eleventh dimension

---

[100] Like this paragraph.

equations - and notice I'm not mentioning any names here - but you really should cut it out. You borrowed the Eleventh dimension from the Membrane guy and while I understand that you were drinking at the time, honestly, fair is fair. The Eleventh dimension was Rudolph's idea and you have to make sure he gets the credit for that. You'll feel a lot better about yourself if you just let it go.[101]

Now, before we begin studying Edgar, I think we should take a moment to review what we have learned so far. We know that there are twelve primary dimensions, operating in reality in groups of three. We have the super-set of space, with the sub-sets of "forward and backward," "up and down," and "left and right." We have time, also a super-set and also with the sub-sets of "forward and backward," "up and down," and "left and right." Finally, we have state, another super-set with the same three sub-sets.

The one constant running throughout the heart of each of these is relativity. So you can think of yourself as existing in a specific locus in space, a specific locus in time and a specific locus in state. With a little practice you can understand that those loci are in fact relative to one another and as a result you can begin to move about freely.

Just remember that each of these loci are in constant flux and in fact might as well have a "no

---

[101] This paragraph is an excellent example of the Microsoft/microscope conundrum.

loitering" sign posted on them. This is important because velocity is a critical part of this equation.

I don't mean to spring velocity on you all of a sudden, as if it's leaping out from behind a tree or something. But we are continually experiencing velocity in all the super-sets of dimension. We are always moving in space, always moving in time and always moving in state. While relativity is constant, our velocity varies from one super-set to another.

If this is still confusing, don't worry.[102] It is important, before we go running full pelt into "Edgar," that we be clear on Space, Time, State, and both relativity and velocity. If you are from New Jersey,[103] please feel free to skip ahead a bit.

For the rest of us:

Relativity in Space:
Imagine yourself in a void, just kinda floating there.[104] You begin moving forward. Sadly, your forward momentum is completely imperceptible to you since there is no point of reference for you use to perceive the movement. You see, in order for you to perceive the movement yourself, you need something to move "in relation[105] to." You need some kind of fixture or object.

---

[102] It never gets any easier, but worrying won't help at all.
[103] Or if you are *like* someone from New Jersey.
[104] Nice, isn't it?
[105] Thus "relativity." See? Science isn't all that hard.

Newton insists it be him... so ok... There's Newton. He remains stationary as you continue moving. From his perspective, you seem to be laying down and moving upward, though in fact you are moving forward.[106] To you of course it seems like it is Newton that is moving and in fact it seems that he is sinking downward.[107] In order to get our bearings we need another point of reference.

Spock. So Spock shows up.

With Spock and Newton as points of reference, you now feel as though you are indeed lying down and so you rotate to bring yourself into alignment with them. And you stop moving for a minute.

There, perfect. See? That's spatial relativity in a nutshell. You can play around with spatial relativity for a few moments and pretend you can fly at the same time.

Fly closer to Newton[108] while noting that[109] when you do so, you fly further from Spock. Then, when you reverse and fly closer to Spock, note that[110] you move further from Newton.

---

[106] We know this mostly because saidI said so earlier.
[107] But this would probably just confuse things, so don't think about that.
[108] And tickle him.
[109] Newton is quite ticklish. See how he's giggling and telling you to cut it out?
[110] Spock does not react to the tickling at all and consequently this is nowhere near as much fun.

Relativity in Time.
You will begin moving forward in time now and
for the sake of clarity in space as well. You move
forward at a rate of one inch per second. Let's do
this for three seconds.

One, one thousand,

Two, one thousand,

Three, one thousand.

Okay stop.

Imagine that each time you said, "one thousand,"
a period appeared on the page.

. . .

Excellent! Are you starting to see it now? Each
of those periods represents one specific locus in
space and in time simultaneously. It makes no
difference if you measure those increments in
inches or seconds, the point is they are relative to
one another because of your velocity of one inch
in space per second in time.

You can move back and forth between those
periods and nothing changes except your locus in
space and time and how your position relates to
the other two positions.[111] This is what is known
as a twin locus. You have your spatial locus

---

[111] Strangely, none of this is on a driver's test.

which is determined by analyzing your vectors along the three spatial subsets and your temporal locus, which is determined by analyzing your vectors along the three temporal subsets.

This determination allows you to say with complete clarity that you are in fact, on your toilet[112] and on Sunday[113] morning.

Relativity in State

To demonstrate this we need to convert those periods to numbers. We, however, will not alter their positions in space or time. That would look very much like this:

1 2 3

We've assigned the value of one to locus 1 in space and locus 1 in time, and have done the same for two and three. You with me so far? Good, good.

Notice how your state changed as you moved between the points. Notice the differences from state 1 to 2 to 3. At state 1 you had "just begun," at state 2 you were "totally hauling ass" and at state 3 you were "about to stop." The three states of "just begun" "totally hauling ass" and "getting ready to stop" are each again relative to one another as well as being relative to each specific locus in time and space.

---

[112] Where I expect this book is likely to be both stored and read.
[113] Don't you wish you'd gone to church to do the whole "Flip Wilson" thing?

What's key here is that all of these are happening all at once within the same "sphere" we call reality or if you prefer, "The Universe."

Within the universe, you are constantly moving in space and time and state. It's simply a matter of velocity. When you realize that velocity is not a fixed rate, but rather is also relative and ultimately variable, then you are beginning to be ready to understand the tenth eleventh and twelfth dimensions.

So it may seem that you can move in space on foot, running, which if you are really fit might be a little less than mile a minute, or super fast like on a rocket ship, a jet aircraft or by letting William drive.[114] Your rate in time might equal one second per second, but your rate in space can be altered. Likewise, your rate in space can remain a constant, while your rate in time is accelerated, decelerated or even reversed. This is also true of state. An example of a rapid acceleration in state might be a "quantum leap," where suddenly your understanding of the world around you changes. Your rate in space and time remain constant, but suddenly your state of being is altered dramatically. Likewise you can decelerate and even reverse in state.[115]

---

[114] William is my wife or my husband, or my "abomination unto Gawd," depending on how you look at it.
[115] I'll leave what that might look like to your own imagination.

Of course, we are not limited to velocity in a single dimension. Point-in-fact, velocity is a universal constant[116] and is relative from one dimensional superset to the next. Consequently as your velocity in space increases, your velocity in time increases[117] relative to everyone else's velocity in both space and time.

It is likely that we can *intentionally* achieve an accelerated rate in any or all combinations of space, time and state. How far you personally experiment with this theory is of course up to you; however I'd recommend some caution. For example, achieving heightened velocity in all three spatial sub-sets simultaneously is also referred to as exploding and is generally considered unhealthy. Fortunately, there do seem to be some safety mechanisms built into the universe to prevent such things from happening casually.

You may be wondering: "How can any of this possibly matter? Even if it is true, how does it change anything?"

In response, I might ask you, how the concept of "up" might alter the experience of life for your average flatlander?[118] When you consider that the concept of "up" leads eventually to things like airplanes and other gadgets, the relevance of understanding *reality* starts to become clear.

---

[116] As well as being a variable.
[117] Making the movie "Planet of the Apes" completely plausible scientifically.
[118] No, not people from the Midwest.

Fortunately you do not have to rely on me, or upon the Science of Theoretics to define reality for you. You can join one of many fine religions that will explain everything for you in a nice tidy and easily digestible form.[119]

Alternately of course, you can try poking at the universe with a stick for yourself whereupon you might conclude that thunder is the angels bowling. As a reality that might not seem half bad, provided of course that you enjoy bowling and in any case it's certainly better than the whole penis/vagina obsession.

Finally of course, you can turn to the solid and ultimately self satisfied[120] scientific community.

While preachers seem to be in abundance,[121] scientists seem like a rare breed. Everyone seems to know someone who has seen Bigfoot, or a UFO, or even a homosexual or two, but most people don't know any scientists.

This has led to the erroneous belief that scientists live in "their ivory towers" casting down dictates of some kind, and spending their days alternately playing god and thinking of ways to make

---

[119] You're bad. Very, very bad, and you deserve everything that happens to you. Also… Gawd loves you so long as you keep your hands off your penis and/or vagina.
[120] If often a bit nerdy.
[121] Due to low testing standards.

religious people look stupid.[122] Scientists do not
live in ivory towers, they live in New Jersey.
New Jersey is crawling with 'em.

I don't mean to say that *all* scientists live in New
Jersey, of course. If you find yourself suddenly in
need of a sociologist, Chicago is the place to
look. Likewise, if you are having trouble with
your rocket, you might consult someone at the
Jet Propulsion Laboratory in California. But... if
you need to get down and dirty with a quantum
physicist, then it's New Jersey for sure.

In New Jersey, you can't swing a dead cat
without hitting a quantum physicist, someone
who works for a quantum physicist, or someone
who knows someone who works for quantum
physicist and so on. If you don't believe me, just
try it.[123]

Once you've located a quantum physicist, he will
likely begin babbling nearly incoherently about
the eleventh dimension and the big bang. If you
can calm him down enough and manage to get
him to speak coherently you'll find that it's
actually quite an astounding story.

---

[122] Mon, Wed, and Fri: Make religious people look stupid.
Tues, Thurs: Dictates. Sat: Play God, then cocktails at Dee
Dee's house.
[123] You probably shouldn't, but if you decide (of your own
volition of course) then the laws of probability dictate that
the closer to Princeton you get, the greater your chance of
success. Please note that it is *not* necessary to bring your
own dead cat as there are plenty of vendors on every street
corner and their prices are quite reasonable.

Apparently a group of quantum physicists were attending a conference in Prague or someplace very much like Prague.[124] Three of the fellows decided to take the train to see some play or something. So there they are, rattling along on the train, playing hooky since it was likely to be a dull conference anyhow,[125] drinking and doing what quantum physicists do on their time off.[126] Just for giggles, one of them decided to include the *lunatic* idea of an eleventh dimension as proposed by Rudolph.[127]

You see, Rudolph espoused an idea that perhaps string theory wasn't all it was cracked up to be and that perhaps instead of "Strings," we ought to be paying more attention to "Membranes." String theory goes to ten dimensions and just stops, leaving you with an unfortunate count of five strings instead of just the one you need to prove that the universe started with a big bang. But Membranes go to eleven![128] Of course this is wildly absurd and was naturally met with a good deal of resistance.[129]

Consequently, Rudolph wasn't often welcomed in Prague and even when his invitation didn't get lost in the mail, his presentations about

---

[124] Such as Vienna, Venice, Versailles, England or someplace else like Prague.

[125] It was "String Cheese Day." Apparently someone thought this was funny.

[126] Math.

[127] Not his real name.

[128] Thank you Spinal Tap!

[129] Primarily by people who had just received a large "string oriented" grant.

Membranes were often met with snickers and the occasional word "bullshit" disguised as a cough. He found it difficult to get grad students to work in Membrane because of course once you've worked in Membrane you'll *never* get a job in String.

So Rudolph, like his namesake, sloshed his way through the slush or whatever brown gunk that counts as slush in New Jersey and hunkered down, feeling very much like Doctor Daystrom.[130] While it is unclear if he also began designing screwy-drill-type things for *his* Impala, or if he managed to round up a few minions and began building his lair, unbeknown to him a foggy Christmas Eve was fast approaching.

The "foggy" part was brought about by the scotch or bourbon or whatever they were drinking that day on the train. I guess it may have been close to Christmas Eve as well.[131] As I mentioned, just for giggles, one of them decided to include the lunatic's idea of an eleventh dimension in his recreational mathematics. While his fellows looked on saying things like: "Oh my God, he's really doing it," and giggling uncontrollably, something amazing happened.

The math worked out.

---

[130] Star Trek: Episode 53: The Ultimate Computer.
[131] Relatively speaking. It was either closer to Christmas past or Christmas future.

You're probably wondering: "What does this mean, the math worked out?" or "Yeah, so?" or perhaps even, "Can we hurry this up?"

Simply put this means that by including the eleventh dimension in the equations, those three inebriated AWOL quantum physicists were suddenly looking at mathematical proof that the big bang had actually occurred.

It means that the big bang wasn't something that the scientists *think* may have happened, it is something that they know has *in fact* happened. In other words, the Pliocene era is not a conversation piece for God, the edge of the world is not further from Spain than we thought and our universe was brought about by a mathematically proven event and not magically, as was previously supposed by roving ministers and other hucksters.

Just then another amazing thing happened. The three quantum physicists were *not* arrested by train authorities even though they were whooping and hollering, leaping about and frightening small children.[132]

Sometime later *another* utterly amazing thing happened. The fact that this discovery had occurred, and a full explanation of all of the ramifications including the potential for all the various gadgets and improved standards of living

---

[132] Later, the scientists checked the math and it was still working out - even though they were sober!

associated with such massive leaps in science was *not* reported on the news.

Well, okay, I don't tend to watch the news much since the 2004 election, but c'mon why wasn't this plastered all over the front page of every newspaper and every TV set in the world? This is, without a doubt, the biggest and most important discovery since *fire*. I mean this is a big deal. So big, it knocks gravity down a peg or two.

What does this have to do with the fact that there are at least 12 dimensions not just the eleven, and why should we name it "Edgar" instead of "Rudolph?"

The fact of 12 dimensions is not so much a fact as it is an implied fact. It is implied because String theory, Membrane theory[133] and of course the Science of Theoretics all have demonstrable evidence that in fact a 12th dimension is likely.

String and "M" both are able to show calculations that extend to the big bang and beyond. What this means simply is that when you get to the big bang, "Whups, watch the edge, there's something else on the other side."

In terms of the Science of Theoretics a 12th dimension is required by The law of Holistic Analog. Since the dimensions operate in packs of three, with all of that up/down pairing and all,

---

[133] Recently renamed "M Theory" by Rudolph for copyright purposes.

having a universe that goes 3/3/3/2 doesn't make any sense at all. Remember the atoms and solar systems analogy? Same deal here.

Finally we come to the naming of this last "primary dimensional super-set" as Edgar. This is achieved through the skillful employment of the Law of Allowable Digression.

Back in the 1930s or so, there was this guy who discovered the 12th dimension. His name was Edgar. Edgar used to go into trances and do some easily dismissible things like healing people and discovering dimensions and the like. Among the many things he mentioned while in one trance or another was that there was life in the vicinity of Jupiter and that life existed primarily in the 12th dimension.[134] That's probably not exactly what he said, but thanks to the Law Of Point I don't have to go and look it up.

If you want to know *exactly* what he said, go ahead and look it up on the Internets.[135] In case you haven't already guessed, his name was Edgar Cayce.

Snort if you like, but the fact remains that Edgar Cayce discovered the 12th dimension and alluded to the fact of life in that dimension just as surely as we live in the third dimension.

---

[134] Once again, relatively speaking, Europa, being a moon of Jupiter, is fairly close to Jupiter. It's certainly close enough to be considered "in the vicinity of."

[135] I know, I know. But our President uses the plural so I thought I'd give it a shot.

Therefore, as America was named for Amerigo Vespucci[136] and the comet that banged into Jupiter was called Schumacher-Levy 9, so too must the 12th dimension and its affiliated 11th and 10th, be named "Edgar."

By the way, I love the fact that you can leap nearly a century forward just by taking something akin to a nap. Isn't state wonderful? I mean really, how *cool* is that? Of course, if you plan on hanging around in the third dimension all the time, then you need all that math and stuff, but still, state is pretty damn cool.

If you'd like, go ahead back, and re-read paragraph one. It should all make sense now.

---

[136] Today, I suspect it would have been named "Vespucciland."

Questions for Discussion

1) What does "Edgar" mean to you now? See! State! Fun, isn't it?
2) Young people tend to drive very fast. Old people tend to drive very slowly. Considering the relationship between velocity and time, do you think this is a coincidence?

Chapter 09
Understanding Edgar

The universe is in fact one coherent whole, comprised of matter and energy[137] traveling relativistically along compatible vectors in space, time, state and Edgar. At first pass, it may seem as if the very idea of Edgar is incomprehensible. In its natural state, Edgar fully exists at all loci in space, time, and state. This does not set it apart from space, time, and state as space, time, and state also exist at all locus of space, time, and state, and Edgar for that matter.[138]

---

[137] Which, like everything else, is in fact the same thing differentiated only by state.
[138] This is the "whole" part, although so far I don't feel I have managed the "coherent" part so well.

We, as individuals, also exist at all locus of space, time, state and Edgar. Our ability to perceive and measure our placement within these dimensions, as well as our ability to manipulate and utilize these dimensions is governed by the flexibility of our locus in Edgar.[139] A higher velocity in state produces greater flexibility and consequently increased utility in Edgar, while a lower velocity produces a greater rigidity or even stagnation.[140]

Conversely, greater velocity in time reduces velocity in state. That is to say, greater velocity in space leads to greater velocity in time. Greater velocity in time folds back upon itself slowing velocity in state. This extra energy is not lost, but instead flows into Edgar, building in pressure and rigidity, and like a balloon filling with air, reducing flexibility in Edgar. This is necessary to maintain dimensional parity.[141]

If you were to reduce your velocity in space, your velocity in time would also slow.[142] At a certain point, the energy from these reductions builds to a critical mass and flows over into state, which accelerates and in turn produces greater flexibility in Edgar.

Your velocity in any of these dimensions is naturally influenced by other groupings of

---

[139] This is also known as our locus within the Edgarian membrane.
[140] See the 2004 presidential election.
[141] I hope this helps to clear up some of the confusion.
[142] This is most apparent when sitting in a waiting room.

particles and waves that are also in motion in the corresponding three dimensional subsets. The various fields, macroscopic structures, waves and particles[143] in each dimensional subset help to regulate velocity, or at the very least influence velocity.

For example, let's assume you are currently sitting in your car.[144] Your car[145] is sitting in a garage, which is sitting on a continental plate which is drifting on a vast sea of magma, which oozes, bubbles, burps and flows around what is generally supposed to be a solid iron core. This core and all the rest of the gunk[146] on top of it is spinning and wobbling even as it is slinging or being slung around the sun, which itself is also in motion and so on. Thus, sitting in your car, you are already traveling at a rather substantial velocity[147] through space.

This pre-existing and significant spatial velocity provides a temporal velocity of one second per second. Were you able to advance your velocity in space by a factor of ten, your velocity in time would advance to a rate of ten seconds per second.[148] You with me so far? Good.

---

[143] And all that other stuff.

[144] Please do not try this experiment at home for reasons that should become self-evident.

[145] Which we may imagine to be a fiery red Ferrari, or if you are a more conservative type, a beige Volvo wagon.

[146] Ourselves included.

[147] Ask someone from New Jersey for the actual speed.

[148] You may be tempted to ask if this is always a 1 to 1 ratio. It's a fair question, but let's not get ahead of ourselves.

Your car cannot add a significant amount of
velocity to the existing velocity that you are
already experiencing. Its engine is simply not
strong enough to establish sufficient velocity,[149]
however, were we to floor it right then and there
a miniscule amount of spatial velocity would be
added and consequently a correspondingly
miniscule velocity in time would be added. Some
of the factors that would contribute to regulating
your velocity would be inertia, air flow and, of
course, the back wall of the garage.[150]

As with the above example, we can see that just
as there are obstacles in space, there are also
events in time, convergence in state, and
resistances in Edgar.

These can be overcome with brute force or sheer
might, however, as is so often the case, a more
circumspect approach is often preferable as it
leads to a more desirable outcome. So it is that
just as backing slowly out of the garage[151] is akin
to choosing to participate in or avoiding events in
time, surfing convergence in state and slaloming
resistances in Edgar. Further, and quite
importantly, while the obstacles, events,
convergence and resistances all have a direct
relationship to one another, that relationship is
often varied. In its most simplistic form, you
encounter an obstacle, experience an event,
develop a convergence and produce a resistance.

---

[149] Even if it *is* a fiery red Ferrari!
[150] Bet you wish you chose a Volvo now!
[151] Having confirmed that the garage door is indeed open.

An imprecise example of this might be that now having successfully backed out of your garage, you start down your street at a reasonable speed, when suddenly, your neighbor[152] comes careening into the street forcing you to slam on your brakes, and quite naturally honk your horn. He sticks his finger out the window and shouts a profanity at you before rocketing away.[153] You might sit for a moment or even make it all the way to the stop sign at the corner before convergence. Suddenly, convergence occurs and you shout, "Fuck you too!" out the window and after stuttering a few additional profanities, despite the fact that he is now well out of earshot, you decide that there is no way you are going to invite that hypocritical son-of-a-bitch to *your* Fourth of July picnic.

"What are you doing?" asked Newton walking into the living room and biting into a plum.

"I'm trying to explain Edgar," I said, "but I don't think I'm doing such a good job."

"Hmm," he said, chewing, "Did you relate obstacle and event?"

"Of course," I said.

---

[152] The one with the sticker that says "Jesus saves" on his bumper.
[153] Perhaps to pick up his children at bible school.

"Oh," he said holding up a finger, "What about convergence? Did you demonstrate how events bring about an alteration in state?"

I nodded.

"Velocity?" he asked, "Don't forget velocity."

"I haven't," I sighed. "Look, technically everything I've written is correct. It's just missing something. I dunno. Here read it for yourself. You tell me."

Newton leaned over the laptop, dripping plum juice on my shirt in the process and began reading. He scrolled down the page as he read and I watched him expectantly. He snickered at the "back wall of the garage" part as well as the bumper sticker and bible school parts.

"Well," he said, standing up and taking another bite, "it is a bit dry."

He chuckled.

"Unlike this plum," he said wiping his chin.

"Yeah, I don't know what to do," I said. "I need the science parts to explain the context. What good is knowing that you can manipulate Edgar to your advantage, when you don't even know what Edgar is?"

Newton shrugged.

"You could take them along on another of your dimensional journeys," he suggested. "The first trip seemed to go over well."

"I suppose," I said.

"You know," he said slurping juice from the plum, "you should listen to me more closely. I slipped ahead in time just a while back to have a peek, so I know what I'm talking about."

"That doesn't seem very fair," I said, "you should have taken me with you. We are *partners* after all!"

"You're the one that threw the prime directive out the window," he said.

"True," I said.

"In any case," said Newton, "the anecdotes go over far better than all your dry wanderings in artificial science. That's why volume two does much better. So stick with the anecdotes."

"I'm not writing a volume two," I said, "just this one book and that's it."

"Well, you already put an excerpt from volume two at the end of this book," he said.

"I did not," I said.

"You will," he said smiling, "and it will be a lot more fun than this book, since it's more anecdote, and less science."

"Really," I said.

"Yep," said Newton, "Volume two: Religion."

"Oh no," I said, "Not religion. They'll kill me. I mean I can screw around with science all I want and the worst I'll suffer will be a few sneers in Prague and Jersey. But religion..."

"Don't worry about that now," he said, "right now, you need to focus on the task at hand. Show them the usefulness of Edgar, and then wrap it up. We'll hit the whole religion thing together later on."

"No, no, no," I said, "I'm not going to do the religion thing at all."

"Don't worry about it," Newton said.

"Besides I have this great novel I've been working on," I said, "I'd rather do that next."

"That's fine," said Newton, "Whatever you like. Now, back to work."

"I mean it," I said.

"I know," said Newton, "get on with Edgar please."

Chapter 10
Manipulating Edgar
Part 1: Edgar and the Big Yellow Bus

So, as you have seen 1970 was a rather
substantial year for me. I had managed to
alienate my sister, NASA and my father. I had
my first opening dialogues with Newton,
discovered the true twelve dimensional nature of
the universe and experienced time travel, which
frankly was no where near as much fun as I had
expected. Importantly I had also graduated from
the minor league to the big league in that during
the final quarter of the year I would be attending

first grade. I had completed my course of study in Kindergarten[154] and through a logic I cannot to this day fathom, I was now thought well prepared to move on to the more advanced studies offered in first grade.[155]

That is to say, that I'm not certain how Kindergarten had in fact served as any kind of prerequisite to the living hell I was about to enter. For the previous year, late 1969 and through the better part of 1970, School was defined as the place the little bus took me to play with a large group of other children. School was a fun thing that you were *allowed* to do. It was permitted only on certain days and then only for a finite portion of the day.

My sister, who you may remember was one year younger than me,[156] was not allowed such adventure. She was far too immature and undisciplined to move about in the larger world. No, only I had the intellectual acuity and world wise savvy necessary to participate at the Kindergarten level. Little did I know that Kindergarten served as the ultimate in deception.

---

[154] This consisted of building a McDonalds restaurant out of over large cardboard building blocks, eating Graham Crackers and drinking milk that had been warmed on a radiator.
[155] In addition to the more common reading, writing and arithmetic, the first grade curriculum in my school at that time provided advanced studies in subjugation, the eradication of self esteem and of course the introductory course in the personification of pure evil.
[156] And remains so to this day.

Little did I know that it was the ultimate in bate and switch.[157]

It isn't that I didn't have warning. There were signs and portents that early September morning as I prepared for a return to those halcyon days I had known as school. I sat on the edge of my bed, waiting for my mother to tie my shoes and speculating at how I would excel this year.

You see, last year I had done quite well in the subjects of playing and drawing, however I hadn't done as well at sharing and speaking politely to others. In fact I had been chastised for referring to my Kindergarten teacher as an old lady. It seemed rather apparent to me that this was fact, and yet I was assured that "old lady" was an impolite term. This year, I would redouble my efforts.

Newton sat beside me as I bounced my heels against the fabric on the side of the box spring. He put his arm around me in a protective and yet comradely fashion.

"If you keep that up," he said, "you'll tear the fabric and get in trouble."

---

[157] Some other examples of bait and switch include: George H. W. Bush's "*Read my lips. No new taxes,*" George W. Bush's "*No empire building,*" A free credit report which is only free when you purchase three additional credit reports through a recurring subscription service and of course a raggedy old man offering candy to a lone child through the passenger door of a running automobile.

"I thought you liked getting me in trouble," I said.

"That's not true," he said.

"You said it was funny," I snapped.

"It is at that," he said, "but that's not why I'm here today."

I pursed my lips.

"Today is going to be a difficult day for you," he said.

"Why," I quipped, "what are you going to do?"

"Nothing," he said his brow furrowing, "it's just that things are changing today."

"Things are always changing," I said, "because of that trophy thing."

"Entropy," he said, "yes but, I mean no..."

Mom walked into my bedroom. She had been in the nursery, where my brother, not even a month old yet had been wailing and carrying on. His behavior has improved significantly since then, however his contributions to the family at that point had been minimal to put it in its best light, and yet Mom continually told him how sweet and wonderful he was. It seemed anachronistic to me at the time since she looked so very tired, but apparently Mom liked being awakened for beverages during the wee hours.[158]

"You look very handsome today," she said. "and I'm very proud you got yourself dressed for school all by yourself."

I blushed deeply, and tried to shrug free of Newton but he hugged me tight to his side.

As was most often the case Mom paid Newton no attention. I was tempted to assume that she could not see him. But, there were those moments when she seemed almost to know. It wasn't so much that she appeared to be aware of him specifically, just that she seemed to sense the presence of something other. Like the faint whiff of perfume in the air, he was to her indistinct; a scent strong enough to notice, but not coherent enough to follow. [159]

I can't tell you exactly what Mom said to me while she tied my shoes, since Newton was sticking out his tongue at me, and rolling his eyes and making funny faces. Under normal circumstances I wouldn't find such behavior funny at all, but if any of you have ever been someplace where laughing is strictly forbidden, well then you know how even the most ridiculous things seem uproariously funny.

For example, in the future, my sister and I would be attending Roman Catholic Sunday School,

---

[158] I made note of this for future reference.
[159] Like many aspects of this book.

together with a largish number of other
unfortunate children. We would be sitting in the
vast marble splendor of the Italian-built church,
golden candlelight flickering and illuminating
the deep rich tapestries and statuary that adorned
the magnificence of the place.

There were forty of us, or perhaps more, attended
by five or six nuns, half of which were thin as
rails with long suffering gaunt faces. The other
half, round like beach balls, with broad false
smiles and childlike cheery voices that somehow
reminded me of daggers thrust into some
unsuspecting persons back.[160]

These poorly chosen PR folk of all things divine
were charged that day with teaching us the "Hail
Mary."[161]

The Hail Mary is a very short prayer being only
two verses long. We were learning it by
repeating it over and over, each in turn reading
from our own personal mimeographed page. A
nun would point, and whoever she pointed at
would read.

Naturally, no matter how much the nuns
glowered or gestured with their hands that we
should slow down, each of us loathed the coming

---

[160] These were the female representatives of the almighty
God on earth in the days of my youth.

[161] If you are not Roman Catholic, then I feel constrained to
point out that the "Hail Mary" is a prayer which in no way
has anything at all to do with football. In fact,
mysteriously, it doesn't even mention football.

of our turn, and once begun wanted it to end as quickly as possible. Consequently, we read very, very fast and occasionally stumbled over a word or two.

During my sister's turn, and rocketing into the second verse which reads: "Holy Mary, Mother of God," my sister, becoming momentarily tongue tied, said: "Hairy Mary, Mother of God."

In all fairness, I tried to contain my laughter. I pressed my lips together, but the laugh came up and filled my cheeks, and a moment later I made a sound more appropriate to my opposite end. The combination of the "Hairy Mary" and the sound of artificial flatulence was more than any child could bear. There was pandemonium in the church. There were gales of laughter, as forty or more children wailed and rolled, and Tim, who you will meet shortly, laughed so hard his nose began to bleed.

There were punishments, of course. This was inevitable. I don't remember exactly what mine was, but I seem to remember being forced to memorize the "Our Father"[162] and having to recite it from memory the following week. Of course, this may have been the result of some other infraction. I'm not sure to this day if I was preternaturally predisposed to locating infractions, or if church was simply a minefield of the things.

---

[162] A significantly longer prayer.

"Newton?" I asked. "What is a polite way to say old lady?"

Mom had left my bedroom at that point, urging me to hurry downstairs.

"You don't want to be late and miss the bus on your first day," she had said.

Newton looked at me for a moment, seemingly puzzled.

"Why do you want to know?" he asked.

"Last year I told Mrs. Q.[163] that she was a nice old lady and I got in trouble."

"I see," said Newton.

"I want to do better this year," I said.

"Fair enough," he nodded. "Anus. The word you are looking for is Anus."

I looked at Newton suspiciously. That answer came too easily.

"Good morning," Newton said, walking into the living room, "I hope you don't mind, I've let myself in."

I looked up from my laptop and nodded.

---

[163] Her initial has been changed to protect the innocent.

"How's things?" I asked.

"Fair, fair," he said brightly.

"You seem awfully cheery this morning," I said.

"What's not to be happy about?" he asked. "It's a beautiful day, the air is cool, the sun is warm and all is right with the world."

"So what happened?" I asked. "C'mon, out with it."

He seemed about to protest for a moment, but then:

"Well, since you asked," he said, bustling over and perching on the arm of my chair. "Madame Curie has agreed to have dinner with me tonight."

"I thought she was seeing Sam Clemens," I said.

He clapped his hands together and leapt up.

"She was, she was," he said gleefully, "but she's decided to play with the big dogs."

"The big dogs?"

He paused a moment, looking back at me over his shoulder.

"It's a euphemism," he said, "it indicates a more mature or superior grouping."

"I know what it means," I said, "I just can't imagine why you are saying it."

"What are you working on?" he asked.

"Edgar," I said. "I'm taking your advice. I'm going back to September of 1970 and taking them along for the ride. Once I'm settled in, I'll show them how to manipulate the Edgarian membrane."

"Sounds like a good plan," he said, "need any help?"

"Nah," I said, "You go ahead and get ready for your date."

He rubbed his hands together briskly.

"I think I'll acquire a new wig," he said, "maybe one of those nice white ones like Thomas Jefferson has."

"Oh," I said, "one question before you go."

He looked at me expectantly.

"Why didn't you go to school with me?"

"Why in the world would I want to do that," he said, "It was a horrible place."

"I know, but I could have used your help," I said.

"Knowing what you know now," he said, "would you have gone if you didn't have to?"

"No, I suppose not," I said, "but you could have given me some warning."

"I did," he said.

"All you did was stand in the door as I left," I said.

"Be strong, be strong," Newton said, leaning out and holding the screen door open for my mother and I.

Mom paused for a moment, clearly perplexed by the strange behavior of the screen door. Newton immediately realized his mistake. He let it go and it banged me in the nose.

Mom and I walked down the driveway to wait for the bus. She held my left hand, and in my right I held the brown paper bag that contained sufficient provisions for my adventure. That being one peanut butter and jelly sandwich wrapped in wax paper, and a supply of vanilla cream cookies, which, despite my promises to the contrary, I intended to eat just as soon as the house was out of view.

My clothes were considerably bigger than was necessary. My over-long pants bunched up over my over-large shoes. The waist of my jacket hung nearly to my knees, and the jacket sleeves covered my hands to the fingernails. This of course was the mandatory outfit of all first graders.[164] In fact, I have noticed since, that it is nearly a school uniform, without regard to any individual school.

The bus, having completed its loop around the town reservoir, now rose into sight at the top of the hill, and began its descent toward the end of our driveway.

Mom squatted down and, using a paper napkin, wiped away the viscous fluid that my nose decided to discharge for some unknown reason.

"You have a good day," she said, "and when you come home, you can tell me all about it."

She wet an alternate corner of the napkin with saliva, and wiped away any remaining dried residue. I smiled at her and nodded.

"Okay," I said.

She hugged me as the bus doors opened with a squeal.

In later years, such hugging would be forbidden, not because I didn't appreciate and enjoy it, but because it resulted in jeers and cat calls from the older children. Today, however, those older children were in a state of shock. Last June, they had been released, freedom loosed upon them, their souls soaring in delight. Little did they

---

[164] Due I'm told to the formula: CSCxCRG or "cost of school clothes" multiplied by the "child's rate of growth"

know that in such a short period of time, their parole would be revoked. They sat, their eyes sunken deep into their sockets as the specter of second grade, or perhaps even, for those surviving few, third grade loomed threateningly before them.

I took my seat and waved back to Mom. I watched and waved until she was out of sight. I felt a pang of sadness. She seemed so lonely to me. I imagined her walking back up the driveway and going back into the house. I imagined the smells and sights and feelings of the place. For a moment, I wanted to be there instead. I considered standing up and requiring the bus to stop. I would get off the bus, and run back up the street, careful to hold up my pants and avoid an embarrassing moment. I would burst into the kitchen. Mom would be surprised, but she would smile when I told her that I decided that I'd rather stay here with her.

But, then instead, there were the cookies; their siren call strong and cloying. White cream pressed between two golden cookies with ornate, neat floral patterns impressed upon their surface. The momentary distraction had been enough. The kitchen was now out of reach. The bus had moved beyond the stop sign at the end of the street. The stop sign was the limit. It was the border of the territory I was allowed to walk. It was too late.

"Ah well," I sighed, reaching into the bag.

"My name is Tim."

I turned. In the seat behind me was a pale sickly looking boy. His hair was so blond, it was nearly white. His skin was pale except for the deep dark circles around his eyes. His eyes were a funny shade of blue that gave them an almost alien appearance. He was thin. It was almost a scary kind of thin.

"Hi," I said, "want a cookie?"

I pulled one of the four cookies from my lunch bag and offered it to Tim. He seemed for a moment to go paler and then threw up.

It wasn't a great gush, as was my experience with the act in the past. Instead, the totality of Tim's vomit was just a mouthful, little more than a burp really; a burp that produced a small steaming white lump that Tim gingerly disgorged onto the back of my seat, almost like an offering.

The material itself was tubular in nature, and apparently composed primarily of solids. I was suddenly engulfed in a smell that was not entirely dissimilar to that of macaroni and cheese.

I felt my gorge rise and I turned abruptly away as I was fairly certain that I could feel a corner of toast with a dab of jelly on it at the back of my throat. Through an act of will, I forced all these fluids back into their proper containers.

"Have you finished yet?" asked Newton.

"No," I said looking up from the laptop, "I'm still on the bus."

"Oh yes, Tim," he said, "Poor boy. Drooled a lot as I recall."

He turned about, modeling his Jeffersonian wig.

"What do you think?" he asked.

"Well," I said, trying to be diplomatic, "that's a new look for you."

"Pretty avant-garde, wouldn't you say?" he asked, taking a formal bow, right leg extended.

"Well," I said, "I think I like your old wig a bit better. It's more ummm.... you."

"Humph," he said, "speak plainly, man, I'm not some delicate flower."

"It's just that with that wig on, you look more like someone named Phineas Fogg, Minister of Plattsburgh First Church of God than Isaac Newton, scientist."

"Extraordinaire," I added hastily.

"Hmmm," he said, studying himself in the full view mirror by the door. He turned his head from one side to the other.

"I see what you mean," he said, a moment later. "My first thought was that this wig would make me appear to be a man ahead of his time, a sentiment physicalized which has oft been attributed to me."

I closed my eyes and nodded.

"I can see now that is not so," he said, "it's missing something."

"Put on your other wig, so you can compare," I suggested.

"Ahh, I have it," said Newton, "A moustache. That would round out the image."

He turned to me and winked.

"I hear that Madame Curie liked old man Clemen's moustache," he said. "Although, for the life of me, I can't imagine why."

I blushed.

"I have a dear friend who is a performer," said Newton. "He has a moustache that can be attached with some spirit gum. I'll ask if I can borrow it, I'm sure he won't mind."

"Newton, I think..." I said.

"I'm off to the Barnum and Baily compound," he said, heading for the door. "I shall return shortly."

He started off, but then paused at the door.

"How's that Edgar thing coming along?"

"It seems to be running a bit long now," I said. "Of course, your interruptions aren't helping."

"Well, just skip ahead a bit," he said.

"I can't really do that," I said, "You know the experiential qualities are critical."

"That's true," he said. "I have it. Stop right here and move on to a new chapter."

"You think?"

"That way you can keep going, give them a chance to grab a snack or go to the bathroom, and in the end, it will make it seem less tedious to them."

"Ok," I said. "Good idea."

Chapter 11
Manipulating Edgar
Part 2: Living Hell

It was September, 1970. The air was crisp and cool and you could see your breath on the air. If you were like me, you could take a deep breath and pretend you were Superman. Using my magnificent Kryptonian lungs, I generated a powerful wind that foiled the bank robbery, and blew the robbers into the waiting arms of a relieved constabulary.

Other classmates chose instead to be massive dragons, which could destroy entire villages in one great and powerful exhalation. I experimented with this on occasion, but didn't experience as much satisfaction at the screams of the villagers at my approach, in contrast with the cheers of a grateful Metropolis.

The bus had delivered me, the other children and Tim's breakfast to the Bielfield Elementary School.[165]

Me, Tim and the other children disembarked and were conducted to the playground at the rear of the school. The fate of Tim's breakfast was left in the hands of the bus driver.

Some of my friends had already arrived. Barry, Mark and Stephanie were there, as was Stanley, my arch nemesis.

Stanley was fat, or should I say, fatter than me. I was dark, he was blond. When we played World War II with our army men, Stanley always played the Nazis. He had small pig-like eyes and even an upturned nose adding to the pig-like appearance.

Later in life, after having been exposed to Darwin's ideas regarding evolution, Stanley was one of the examples I cited in my paper on the possibility of multiple vectors of evolution. It

---

[165] Bielfield, in ancient Sanskrit means, ruler of the unholy nether regions.

was my assertion that life reasserted itself on Earth, not through a single vector of evolution wherein Homo sapiens evolved exclusively from chimpanzees, but rather through multiple vectors, leading to a significantly wider variety of mutations. Consequently some Homo sapiens, like Stanley, might have evolved from pigs, while others, like me, might indeed have evolved from baboons. Still others may have evolved from gorillas, frogs, horses and in fact, I posited, that perhaps the sheer diversity of life itself infers that multiple vectors would have been in play.

Stanley also thought Thor was a better super hero than Superman. Doofus!

More children were arriving, quite literally by the bus load. The trap had not yet been sprung, but the teachers stood by their classroom doors quietly chatting so as not to give away their dark purpose.

So far everything seemed perfectly fine. It hadn't dawned on me that the morose, stunned and in some cases zombie-like behavior of the older children should have served as an indicator that something foul was afoot. But like Mom noticing the screen door then dismissing it, this was, I assumed, a fluke. Also, I was distracted at that moment by Stanley who was once again dredging up that lame argument that Thor was better than Superman because Thor was a real god, and Superman was just made up.

"They don't make comic books about real people," I argued, certain that such an overt fact would put an end to this non-sense once and for all.

"Yes they do," he said.

"Nuh-unh," I replied.

'Doo too," he said.

"Nuh-Unh," I repeated.

"Well, they did about Thor," he said. "My grandpa says that Thor is the real god of the German people. Also you're stupid, cause you're Italian."

He had a point. I was Italian. I still am too. But I was too young to call him on injecting a non-sequitur statement into the debate. I didn't know how to object, but I could sense that it was somehow a break in the rules. So instead, I said, "That's stupid."

"You're stupid," he said.

This continued for some time. We sent accusations of stupid back and forth like it was a badminton match. Stanley's face grew red during this. His complexion was prone to it. Even the slightest upset caused vast pink splotches to appear across both his cheeks. Also, when he got angry, he furrowed his brows making his already tiny eyes appear even smaller. He would bunch his fists and draw up his shoulders as he grew more and more furious. This among other things, contributed to his gaining the nickname "Stanley the Tank," well before the end of second grade.

The bell rang.[166]

We clustered around door three, as that was to be our new room. Others clustered around other doors. Five, seven and so on. They were greeted by teachers who ushered them into the numbered rooms. Our door, however, remained closed. It was tall and windowless. It was metal. It was blue, with a bright yellow number three stenciled on it. It stood stark and immobile against the barren concrete block wall.

Just as I had begun to suspect that perhaps we had made some kind of mistake, there was a sound from behind the closed door. It was a sound, more like a chunk than a click. The door moved slightly, seemed to hesitate for a moment and then ever so slowly began to open.

Shrouded in shadow, standing just beyond the threshold was a woman. Rather, she appeared to be a woman. The truth is, she was... something awful; something wicked in the guise of a woman.

---

[166] I would spend the next twelve years governed by bells. The bells would tell me when to wake up, when to eat, when to think about math and when to think about science. Had I known this then, I think I might have screamed.

She moved forward, slowly, as if cautious of the sunlight. There was silence, broken only by the sound of desiccated scale on scale as she took first one then two steps toward us.

"Oh that's a bit much, isn't it," said Newton.

"Oh, you're back," I said, looking up and forcing myself not to giggle.

Newton was wearing a thin handlebar mustache, much like you would expect a strongman from the carnival to wear. It was jet black and curled out away from the sides of his face looking more like an insect appendage than a growth of human hair.

"No, Newton," I said, standing and setting the laptop aside. "I'm your friend. I can't let you do this."

"What?" he asked incredulously.

"This," I said, tugging on the moustache, an action I immediately regretted. I looked at the slime on my fingers.

"Vaseline," Newton said, "Helps keep the shape."

I looked down at my fingers and rubbed them to massage away the Vaseline.

"Just be glad this isn't the olden days," Newton chuckled. "You wouldn't believe what they used to use."

"I don't even want to know," I said. "You cannot go out on a date with Madame Curie looking like that."

"Why not," he demanded.

"It's completely over the top," I said.

"Oh, like 'desiccated scale on scale' *isn't* over the top," he snapped.

"Alright fine," I said, "but this... this..."

"In fact, that entire paragraph, yes and even the one before that should go," he said, studying the text more closely.

"Don't try to change the subject," I said. "Now, that stupid wig and horrible.... mustache has got to go."

"Fine," he snapped. He pulled off the wig and threw it to the floor. "Happy now?"

"Not completely," I said.

He scowled and gingerly pulled at the mustache. Apparently, the spirit gum was quite sticky and he grimaced as he removed it.

"Better," I said, "Now, where is your wig. You should put that on."

"Why?"

"Because now you look like a white raisin impersonating an ancient Egyptian court magician," I said.

He stomped off, upstairs. There was some temperamental thudding and banging and a moment or two later he returned looking exactly the way *the* Isaac Newton should look.

"That's better," I said. "That's the man I've come to know and love."

"Bah," he said, but I could tell he was feeling a little better. A little flattery always goes a long way with Newton.

"Besides," I said, "Madame Curie should be given the opportunity to enjoy herself in the company of the real you. Otherwise you might find yourself in a relationship where you have to pretend to be someone you are most certainly not. That way leads to tassels and tie die."

"I suppose," he said.

"You are after all the man who has the better part of an entire paradigm named after him."

"That's true," he said drawing himself up. "Indeed that is very true."

He stooped down and began reading from the laptop.

"Hmm, he said, "it seems to me that you are missing the point of this experiment."

"I am not," I snapped defensively.

"The point we are trying to demonstrate is the modification of a pre-existing vortex and its corresponding inflexibility within Edgar."

"Yeah," I said, "So?"

"Well you can't accomplish that by merely describing this poor woman in unflattering terms."

"Poor woman?" I snapped. "She was evil. Pure evil."

"Look here," he said babbing back to Chapter 10, "you encountered and modified a pre-existing vortex and relaxed the rigidity of the surrounding Edgarian membrane right here."

"Where?" I asked.

"Here," he said pointing at the screen, "just before Tim threw up."

"I took my seat and waved back to Mom," he read aloud. "I watched and waved until she was out of sight. I felt a pang of sadness. She seemed so lonely to me. I imagined her walking back up the driveway and going back into the house. I imagined the smells and sights and feelings of the place. For a moment I wanted to be there instead. For a moment I considered standing up and requiring the bus to stop. I would get off the bus, and run back up the street, careful to hold up my pants and avoid an embarrassing moment. I would burst into the kitchen. Mom would be surprised, but she would smile when I told her that I had decided that I'd rather stay there with her."

"Yeah, so what," I shrugged.

"Take a look at membrane before you wrote that paragraph," Newton said.

I took a deep breath and closed my eyes.

"You see it?" he asked.

"Yeah," I said, "but I still don't understand what..."

"Shh," he said, "Now take a look at it after you wrote that paragraph."

"Oh wow," I said, "the vortex is smaller and the rigidity of the membrane is lessened."

"Precisely," said Newton, "Now consider it for a moment. You felt a pang of sadness...she seemed so lonely. What did you do?"

"I wanted to stay home so Mom wouldn't be lonely," I opened my eyes. "Oh my god. Newton, that's amazing!"

"Of course it is," he said, casually throwing up his hand, "it's twelfth dimensional physics."

"So I made my teacher into a monster to give me an excuse to stay home..."

"Oh no!" he said, "She was a monster. The personification of pure evil in fact, but that's not important. What is important is your reaction to her, and more precisely the reasons behind your reactions."

"Newton," I said grasping his arm, "are you telling me that the twelfth dimension is entirely in my head?"

"Don't be an idiot," he said, "and don't go all new age-y on me either and start talking about higher-selves or personal powers or spirit guides."

"Aren't *you* my spirit guide?" I asked.

"Well yes," he snapped, "but that's not the point."

"Well I think it is," I said.

"The point is that this is science," he snapped, "not some hokey mumbo jumbo that requires incense, candles and quartz. It is overt, absolute and can be proven mathematically... well it will be proven mathematically soon. The dimensions and their corresponding sub-sets are all overtly true, they occupy the universe as real substantial forms. They are interconnected and interdependent..."

"Alright alright," I said, "I'm on your side here. It's science."

"And why did you pick the name Edgar," he snapped, "that's a horrible name for this. I mean really, space, time, state…all very descriptive! But Edgar?"

"I was trying to be funny *and* consciousness sounded hokey," I snapped. "Besides, consciousness has the connotation of being insubstantial when in fact, as you have reminded me repeatedly; it has the same substantial qualities as the rest of the dimensions."

"You could have tried some other words," he said, "coalescence, super-state…something!"

"Edgar, let's us say things like 'Edgarian membrane,'" I said, "and *that's* funny!"

"Yes," he said. "yes, it is."

"Good then," I said.

"Well then," he said. "Good."

There was a pregnant pause as I looked at him.

"Alright then," he said, "that's it."

Chapter 12
Conclusion

Before Newton gets here this morning I wanted to take a moment to share with you the story behind Newton and the apple. You see, there was a certain archbishop, and I won't mention his name mostly because the mere mention of his name makes Newton fly off the handle.[167]

---

[167] This is primarily because he antagonized Newton throughout most of his career. He ridiculed Newton frequently, conspired against him... you know the type.

When Newton published the Principia, admittedly the result of decades of hard study and even harder math, this fellow minimized the accomplishment by creating the story of Newton being hit on the head by an apple.[168]

He would tell this story at dinner parties, in the courts of kings, even out behind the stables. Anywhere he felt he could get a laugh. He would always wait just long enough to be sure he had received all the good vibes that someone laughing at a joke you made brought, before bringing it down a notch, like the Bill Murray lounge singer character. He would remind everyone that it was an act of God that led to true greatness and as for the actions of a man, well... eh. So what?

Naturally, this flies in the face of what little we know of God, and while I have many opinions and thoughts on the subject, I think I'll reserve them for volume 2: Religion.[169]

I invented[170] the Science of Theoretics as a way for us to begin to observe and in fact participate in absolutely real phenomena that is currently

---

[168] It seems that he found the idea that it was an apple itself, to be a particularly subtle twist it being a play on the idea of the Tree of Knowledge and all that.

[169] In all honesty I have absolutely no intention of writing that book. But Newton assures me that he's been to the future and I already have. Personally, I'd like to get on with something a little more serious in terms of fiction. But I guess we'll just have to see how things develop.

[170] Made up.

outside the scope of most other established institutions.[171]

The Science of Theoretics will not lead, at least not directly, to starships, warp drive or any of that hard science kinda stuff, but it might help make your journey through the wilderness of life a little more tolerable.

Our universe is vast. The left-right, Up-down, forward-back parts, all true, on all levels of dimension and I guess you could say that Edgar is the key to all the others, but, while kinda true, it's also kinda not.

In the end remember that The Science of Theoretics is experiential and anecdotal. Let the Math guys do the math, that's important stuff too, but let's not give up entirely on non-math based reality either. Play with it, experiment on your own and have a blast. As Newton says: "They're your toes, wiggle 'em if you want."

"Whew," Newton said walking in, "it's raining cats and dogs out there."

He flapped his coat, sending rain water flying in all directions.

"Morning, Newton," I said.

"Morning," he said. "How are you feeling?"

---

[171] Let's not forget that making some money for rent and groceries was also on my mind.

"A little melancholy," I said, "I expected to be glad to be finished with this book... but..."

I shrugged.

"Well there is always volume two," he said.

"I really don't think I want to do that," I said.

"Let's see what you have so far," he said. "Ahh first off, that horse's ass wasn't an archbishop, he was a colleague."

"I know, it just reads better as archbishop, that way I get the pop culture "Bill Murray" thing in there."

"Mmm," Newton said, "I never said anything about toe wiggling."

"I know," I said, "Oh say, how'd your date with Madame Curie go?"

"Not so well, he said.

"Oh oh," I said. "What happened?"

"It started off well enough," he said, "I thought I was doing quite well. Nice restaurant, some flowers, you know?"

"Yep," I said.

"Then she wanted to talk," he said.

I looked at him expectantly.

"I think of myself as an excellent orator," he said.

I dropped my head into my hands.

"I spoke of my youth, my accomplishments; you know all the necessary things. But after a time, she interrupted me."

"How long?" I asked.

"Just before the halfway point," he said.

"Oh my god," I muttered.

"I was just telling her about that dastardly Hooke, and how he tried to claim a part of the Principia simply because he had written me a few sophomoric letters..."

"What did she say?"

"I was right in the middle of describing his loathsome character too, some of my best stuff..."

"Newton," I demanded.

"She asked if I knew her first name."

"What did you say?" I asked.

"I said yes of course," he said.

"And did you?"

"No," he said, "not exactly."

"And by not exactly you mean not at all."

"Precisely," he sighed.

"So what did you do?"

"How would you put it," he said, "I took a shot."

"You guessed?"

"Yes," he said. "I felt I had no other choice."

He paused, and we looked at each other. The moment seemed to stretch out, but finally I said:

"And?"

"I said Genevieve, but that was clearly incorrect as she took the napkin from her lap and made as if to rise. I suppose I panicked at that point," he said. "I began saying names to her, in vain hope that I might strike upon a moment of fortune. Eleanor was my next attempt, but by then she had risen, and had turned away. She hadn't taken more than a step when I called out the name Marie."

"Her name is Marie?" I asked.

"Possibly," he said, "she neither confirmed nor denied."

"Marie Curie," I said, "it kinda rhymes."

"Indeed," said Newton.

"I don't know," I said, "That doesn't sound right to me. Are you sure?"

"I have no idea," said Newton, "at any rate, it caused her to turn back toward me. She regarded me for a moment and then asked what she was most famed for discovering. Of course, I had no clue, so I ventured another guess."

"What did you say?" I asked.

He sighed, drawing himself up.

"I don't suppose that matters," he says, "Apparently, my answer was incorrect or at any rate, insufficient. She left."

"Oh, Newton," I said apologetically.

"No matter," he said, "what's done is done."

"No really," I said, "what did you say?"

"It's far too embarrassing and I don't want it in that book of yours," he said.

"Alright fine," I said. "Just tell me."

He leaned over and whispered in my ear.[172]

---

[172] He said: "Something to do with mold."

Appendix i
<u>About the Author</u>

My publisher and my editor are both imaginary, but somehow they manage to get the job done so kudos to them. My publisher never returns my calls, but he doesn't take any money either so I guess that's fair.

My editor, on the other hand, talks to me constantly. "Oh don't put a comma there," he says, "and this whole sentence should be separated from the rest of the paragraph." In fact, he talks so much about dangling participles, incomplete sentences and all nature of things dull, that I have decided to ignore him for the most part.[173] Like Tim that morning on the bus, I've decided to present you with this … ummm… gift.

I would like to say that, despite appearances to the contrary, this is not my first novel. In fact, I have written three first novels before this first novel.

My first, first novel was horridly bad. I don't mean an average kind of bad. I mean a Bush Administration kind of bad. It was an utter catastrophe! It centered on two aliens who enter an average suburban house to abduct someone but have a variety of problems. It was a slap-stick comedy.[174] I planned to publish this novel under the name John Thomas.[175]

My second first novel was a bit better. This should not be interpreted to mean that it was good, just that it was better than the work of John Thomas. I had matured as a writer and as a human being, and this was reflected in the novel. This novel was a fantasy novel. It was something like Lord of the Rings, with the scope of Star Wars and the universal appeal of Star Trek. At

---

[173] Having read this far, this should be apparent to you already.

[174] One alien was named Y'von, the other named Y'vern. See what I mean? Hilarious!

[175] No, I wasn't joking. I was young. I had no idea that John Thomas was another name for penis.

least, that's how I introduced it to a prospective publisher.

While this story was still not *well* within the spectrum of "good," apparently it was good enough to get my foot in the door. Weeks and weeks of waiting turned into months and months of waiting.

After persistently calling and nagging the publisher,[176] I found that I was one of two new writers under consideration by the publishing house. This of course was back in the day when publishing houses took on new writers and worked with them until they actually wrote something publishable.

They were cordial. They were communicative. They never would tell me who the other guy was so that I could read his book and sneer.

My third first novel has likewise never been published. I consider it, like all of my previous novels, a work in progress. It needs a new ending, a new beginning and the middle needs to be completely reworked. It fits somewhere in the horror genre, but to be honest, it's not an easy fit. It has vampires, both psychic and sanguine, werewolves that are in fact aliens, immortals, ghosts and spirits. It also has some wry humor and something to say about the human condition, though I'd be hard pressed to say just what that might be.

---

[176] Actually the publisher's secretary.

Still though, it's a good story and I'll get around to finishing it one of these days.

I have had one short story published. This makes me an official card carrying author since someone, somewhere, said that to be officially considered an author, you must at one time have been paid by someone for something you have written.

The short story was called "Letters from Home" and was published in ten installments in a magazine in Provincetown Massachusetts. It was a series of letters from a grandmother to her grandson, who had moved to Provincetown. The grandmother always signed her letters with:

Love,
Gram

Older generations read it and laughed and cried. They recognized the character of the grandmother. People of my generation laughed and smiled wistfully, they too recognized the character. People of a younger generation stared blankly at the pages and said..."Who is this dude Graham?" To this day, I am uncertain if this story was a success or not.

Since I became a published author back then, I have been working diligently on becoming a *good* author with an eye toward becoming someday, perhaps even a *great* author. I have observed great authors and have noted their traits and found many of those self-same traits in myself.

For example, like most of the great scientists in history, many great authors have unusual hair. As has been established, I have unusual hair.

Many great authors have had personalities that range from mildly depressed to wildly insane. I fall into that range nicely, being *wildly* depressed and mildly *insane*. A friend of mine once commented that the definition of Psychotic was, in essence, that the way the world works, as defined by a psychotic, is disparate from the way the world really works. By this, I must assume that he meant that the whole world is psychotic, save for me.

Unfortunately, my similarity to great authors more or less ends there. Great authors typically have the benefit of an education at an esteemed university of some kind. I myself have been made handicapped in this regard by having attended a mediocre university.

I also seem to find myself living in a time[177] where thinking and writing is considered a less valuable, or at the very least, an impractical profession. It seems to me that our society tends to agree with my paternal grandmother, who was known to comment often:

---

[177] Called "Modern Times." Coincidence? I think not!

"That's nice. If you like that sort of thing."[178]

Similarly, I developed IFT®[179] relative to my temporal locus in modern times.

In the last years of the twentieth century, everybody seemed to get very excited about "interactivity," as if interactivity was a brand new thing.

Many people sat in their interactive houses, surrounded by their interactive family, and were completely amazed that they could click some blue text on a screen and be whisked from one bit of information to another.[180]

While I certainly enjoy pornography,[181] I felt as if it might be important to remind folks that novels, essays, articles and other book-like things are interactive too. In fact, unlike other media, the written word directs[182] a stream of thought directly to an area of the brain somewhere just behind the prefrontal cortex. This stimulates cognition, which as we know, has been known to lead to the ancient and mythological "idea."

Let's see? What else?

---

[178] This comment was typically accompanied with a facial expression that appeared to me as if someone had packed her left nostril with feta cheese.
[179] Interactive Footnote Technology
[180] Most found that eventually no matter what you clicked you wound up at a site named:
:GirlsGirlsGirlsLiveLiveLiveNudeNudeNude.com
[181] Who doesn't?
[182] Or streams.

Oh yeah. I will be[183] forty-three next month.[184] I smoke way too much[185] and could stand to lose about fifty pounds or so. I enjoy movies and television, and long talks about interesting things.

I guess that's about it.

I wish you well and I'll chat with you again soon.

P.S. Newton says: "Hi."

---

[183] Or have been.

[184] Or last month, or a couple of years ago for that matter.

[185] Yes, tobacco! Jeeze!

Salvatore LoGiudice

Appendix ii
An Excerpt from

And God Said:
"Wanna See Something Funny?"
Vol. 2: Religion

Religion has assigned itself the unenviable task of attempting to determine just what it is that God wants from us. I don't think they've succeeded too terribly well, but I do thank them for trying. Given that like me, they have pretty much made it all up as they went along, it makes their failure understandable.

Early on, religion seemed to think God wanted unswerving obedience. Later, Blood. I don't think there is any evidence to support the idea that God wanted either of those things. I mean think about it... if you made a vacuum cleaner that only sucked when it decided to suck... that would pretty much suck wouldn't it? Also if God wanted blood, he could have just made as much as he wanted without getting us involved in the first place.

If we must try to figure out what God wants to give our lives meaning, then we have to look at what it is we do naturally, and make some conclusions based on that. It is not at all unreasonable to base our ideas regarding what God wants on what it is we do, since the rest of the planet seems to work that way too. Birds do what birds do, flowers do what flowers do and we do what we do.

At first glance, you may be tempted to quantify rather than qualify. That is to say to assign a value based on how much we do something, rather than considering the qualities of the things we do. Granted, we do tend to kill one another, but honestly, you might as well conclude that God wants poop cause we do that a lot more often than most of us kill. Also, if it *was* poop that God was after, He would be much better off with dinosaurs that must have had prodigious nearly epic bowel movements. They were also better equipped for killing as well.

www.ingramcontent.com/pod-product-compliance
Lightning Source LLC
LaVergne TN
LVHW011229080426
835509LV00005B/397